WILL SMITH

A Biography of A Rapper Turned Movie Star

by Michael A. Schuman

 Enslow Publishers, Inc.
40 Industrial Road
Box 398
Berkeley Heights, NJ 07922
USA
http://www.enslow.com

Author's Dedication
To my friends Jon, Lil, And Natale Novak

Original edition published as *Will Smith: "I Like Blending a Message with Comedy"* in 2006.

Library of Congress Cataloging-in-Publication Data

Schuman, Michael.
   Will Smith : a biography of a rapper turned movie star / Michael A. Schuman.
      p. cm.
   Includes bibliographical references and index.
   Includes filmography.
   Includes discography.
   ISBN 978-0-7660-3994-0
   1. Smith, Will, 1968—Juvenile literature. 2. Actors—United States—Biography—
Juvenile literature. 3. African American actors—Biography—Juvenile litera-
ture. 4. Rap musicians—United States—Biography—Juvenile literature. I.
Title.
   PN2287.S612S36 2012
   791.4302'8092—dc23
   [B]
                              2011024347

Future editions:
Paperback ISBN 978-1-59845-397-3
ePUB ISBN 978-1-4645-1148-6
PDF ISBN 978-1-4646-1148-3

Printed in China

062012 Leo Paper Group, Heshan City, Guangdong, China

10 9 8 7 6 5 4 3 2 1

To Our Readers: We have done our best to make sure all Internet addresses in this book were active and appropriate when we went to press. However, the author and the publisher have no control over and assume no liability for the material available on those Internet sites or on other Web sites they may link to. Any comments or suggestions can be sent by e-mail to comments@enslow .com or to the address on the back cover.

Cover Photo: AP Images/Evan Agostini

CONTENTS

Chapter 1

RAPPIN' INTO HISTORY

By the time he was thirteen years old, Will Smith was already known as a rapper on the street corners of Philadelphia. Seven years later, he was up for one of the music industry's highest honors. It was February 1989, and the setting was the annual Grammy Awards ceremony. Grammys are given every year by the National Academy of Recording Arts and Sciences (NARAS) to honor the best performances of the previous year.

Will Smith and Jeff Townes were recording together as DJ Jazzy Jeff and the Fresh Prince. They had been nominated for a Grammy in the category of best rap performance for the song "Parents Just Don't Understand" on their album

The Origins of Rap Music

Rap music first emerged from the African-American neighborhoods of New York City in the late 1970s. The word *rap* was 1960s slang for *talk* or *conversation*. A person could *rap* with friends or get involved in a *rap session* about a certain topic. So it seemed only natural that music with spoken words would be called rap music. According to some entertainment historians, RAP is an acronym for "Rhythm And Poetry."

He's the DJ, I'm the Rapper. The fact that rappers were even being nominated for a Grammy was a major news item.

Rap music had been around for more than ten years, but this was the first time it was being included in the Grammys. The National Academy of Recording Arts and Sciences has always been slow to recognize new genres of music. Although the Grammys were first awarded in 1958, it was not until 1964 that a rock and roll act, the Beatles, won an award. Elvis Presley, the King of Rock and Roll, never won a Grammy for his rock recordings; only his gospel records won Grammys: in 1967, 1972, and 1974. The Rolling Stones, who released their first recording in 1964 and are considered by many critics to be one of the greatest rock and roll bands of all time, did not win a Grammy until 1994.

It is no secret that NARAS is not at the cutting edge of new musical art forms. In 1989, NARAS president Mike Greene described the organization as "a fat old lady walking down the street, and it's easy to throw things at us."[2] That is why it was big news when rappers made it to the Grammys that year.

Some rap music is political and angry, filled with profanity and lyrics that defend violence and demean women. Smith and Townes's rap music, in contrast, is a humorous celebration of topics such as dating and partying. While their style of rap has its roots in the African-American community, young people of all races can relate to the subject matter and humor. Some other rappers have criticized Smith and Townes's music, saying that without the hard edge and anger, it is watered down and not real rap.

There are still some people who do not consider rap to be legitimate music. This group includes many whites and older people, even some of those who had grown up with the rebellion of rock and roll. Although rap was finally making it to the Grammy Awards, it seemed to Smith and Townes that NARAS might have felt the same way. The duo was disappointed to learn that the award for rap performance would not be televised on the live Grammy Awards program.

According to NARAS, this was not a judgment on the validity of one type of music over another. It was simply a question of time. There were seventy-six musical categories, but only fifteen presentations would fit into the broadcast. The other awards, including the one for rap performance, would be given out in a separate ceremony before the broadcast. NARAS president Greene explained, "Every year people get mad because their form is not on. I'm glad people feel passionate about their music. We take note and generally try to even it out year by year."[3]

Still, Smith and Townes took it as a slap in the face. They were proud of their music and proud that it came out of their African-American heritage. Smith explained their frustration, saying, "It's like going to school for twelve years and then not being able to walk across the stage [and get your diploma]."[4]

After thinking it over, Smith and Townes made a decision. If their category of music was not important enough to be televised, then they would boycott the ceremony—and they did. The people of NARAS got the message. After that year, the rap performance award would be televised.

Smith and Townes won the 1989 Grammy for best rap performance. Even though the duo did not attend the ceremony, that night marked the first time that many people heard the name Fresh Prince. It would be far from the last.

Chapter 2

GETTING PAID TO PARTY

Willard Christopher Smith Jr. was born on September 25, 1968, in Philadelphia, Pennsylvania. His parents, Willard and Caroline Smith, both worked full time. Will's father was a refrigeration engineer with his own business, and Caroline was an administrator for the local Board of Education. Their first child, Pamela, was four years old when Will was born.

The Smith family lived comfortably in a mid-sized brick row house in a middle-class section of Philadelphia called Wynnefield. It was a diverse neighborhood, with many African-American and Jewish residents.

From his first days, Willie Jr. was known as a bit of a show-off. In one of the earliest family videotapes, toddler Willie is seen hogging the camera. According to his mother, Will could speak before he could walk. His maternal grandmother, Helen Bright, recognized Will's knack for showmanship and cast him in a variety of religious plays and pageants at the family's church, the Resurrection Baptist Church. Throughout his childhood, Will loved entertaining his family and friends.

When Will was three, his mother gave birth to twins, Harry and Ellen. The family of four suddenly turned into a family of six. But even with two more mouths to feed, Will's parents made sure their children never lacked anything they needed.

Will was a tall, gangly boy with big ears. Some of the other kids told him he resembled Alfred E. Newman, the goofy-looking cartoon mascot of *Mad* magazine. One boy joked that Will's big ears made him look like a car going down the street with its doors open.

Will drew attention away from his looks by playing the class clown. When he was not cracking jokes or making up funny stories, he was doing the typical gross things that boys enjoy—such as stuffing straws up his nose for a quick laugh. When Will was being punished at home, he would make funny faces at Harry and Ellen, making them laugh. Then the twins would get in trouble, too.

Will Smith Sr., who had been a drill sergeant in the United States Air Force, drew upon his military background to instill discipline at home. His family lived by the words "You get up in the morning prepared to go to work."[1]

Will Jr. later said that both his parents had strong beliefs about child rearing. His mother's emphasis was education. She read to Will constantly, and he especially loved the rhyming books by Dr. Seuss. Will's father was a tough disciplinarian. Like many parents at that time, he spanked his children for misbehaving. Will later said that he had little problem with his father's discipline: "It's hard, but not any harder than the world is. I believe in corporal punishment. My father trained good soldiers. I'm ready to deal with whatever life has to offer."[2]

Smith believes it was the partnership of both his parents that motivated him. "Life is about balance," he said. "If my mother wasn't in the house, who knows how I would have reacted to that militaristic upbringing? I had the best of both worlds."[3]

Will's mother wanted her children to get the best schooling available. Even though she worked for the public school system, Caroline Smith thought her son would benefit from a parochial school, where religious values as well as basic learning are emphasized. Although the Smiths are Baptist, five-year-old Will was enrolled in Our Lady of Lourdes, a Catholic school. He was one of the few African-American students at the school.

Will proved to be a good student, doing well in math, science, and English. He loved writing poetry, and his teachers were impressed by his creativity. Will particularly liked to have fun in class, entertaining other kids with his jokes and stories.

At home, the Smith household was filled with music. Everyone in the family sang, and nearly all played an instrument. Will learned how to play piano from his mother and became a skilled, self-taught drummer, too.

Throughout 1976, the United States was celebrating its bicentennial—the nation's two hundredth birthday. Americans were filled with patriotic spirit, and many traveled around the nation visiting famous landmarks. The Smiths were no exception. The family piled into the car for a driving trip across the country and back.

Some sights the Smiths took in were Mount Rushmore in South Dakota, Yellowstone National Park in Wyoming, and the Alamo in Texas. Unlike some children his age, little Will was not bored by these places. In fact, the trip made a lasting impression on him. Years later, Smith said, "When you see something beautiful, something bigger than you, whether created by nature or man, it changes you, it mellows you, it changes your attitude toward life."[4]

Something else that made an impact on Will was an outdoor project that he and his brother, Harry, had to do one year. In their yard was a massive but crumbling brick wall, about fifty feet wide and sixteen feet high. Willard Sr. instructed his two sons to replace the entire wall, one brick at a time. The job included mixing the concrete by hand. At first, the brothers could not believe what their father expected them to do. Will later said, "I remember standing there thinking, 'There is no way I will live to see this completed.' He wanted us to build the Great Wall of Philly! I remember hoping that my father would get committed, because if he were in an insane asylum, then we wouldn't have to finish the thing."[5]

To Will and his brother's dismay, Willard Smith Sr. spent a good part of the summer and fall supervising their building project. The work was drudgery, and it took them six months until the wall was finished. Afterward, Will and Harry were proud of their job, as was their father. Will recalled, "Dad told me and my brother, 'Now don't you all ever tell me you can't do something.' I look back on that a lot of times in my life when I think I won't be able to do something, and I tell myself, 'One brick at a time.'"[6]

In spite of his venture into wall building, Will still preferred music to masonry. When he was about ten, he received a stereo system as a gift from his parents. His favorite record albums—there were no compact discs in those days—were by funk groups.

Will had all sorts of other hobbies, too. He loved sports and admired the basketball stars Wilt Chamberlain and Julius Erving, who played for his hometown Philadelphia 76ers. Will also enjoyed playing chess, a game he had learned from his father when he was just eight years old.

Will was especially fascinated by dinosaurs. He memorized facts about the geological eras in which different dinosaurs lived and thought the most interesting dinosaur was the stegosaurus. He was intrigued by science-fiction stories, too. He later said, "It's not so much as an actor that I love it, just as a kid growing up, science fiction was my genre. I loved the imagination of

Funk Music

Funk was born out of a combination of jazz, soul, and rhythm and blues, three styles of music with roots in African-American communities. Funk music is usually raucous, with a heavy bass line and brassy horn section. Some specialized funk includes rock-and-roll guitar licks. Among the most popular funk artists at the time, and some of Smith's favorites, were the Bar-Kays and Parliament/Funkadelic. Funk reached its peak of popularity in the early and mid-1970s.

science fiction. I think at heart, I'm really an idealist and there's nowhere for me in entertainment that you can really stretch the bounds of human possibility more than science fiction. I just love it."[7]

With his natural curiosity and basic intelligence, Will was able to earn good grades. However, there was another reason he continued to achieve. He later said, "I hated being in trouble. I was so petrified of my parents [that] I managed to avoid most pitfalls teens fall in. . . . My father was a serious disciplinarian. I wouldn't dare bring home a D on my report card. The bottom line was no nonsense."[8] His father's expectations followed Will beyond the classroom: "I never tried drugs," he said, "because I felt he would kill me. Literally."[9]

Although Will Smith Sr. was tough on his children, Will Jr. realized his father was just as hard on himself. He knew that his father always did whatever a job required. Will often went along when his father was installing freezers in supermarkets. One time, when Will was about twelve years old, they were setting up a freezer in a supermarket basement. Across the floor, store employees had spread a rat poison called D-Con.

Will said, "So we go in and [my father] is looking for the compressor and he has a flashlight. And [here] is a dead rat that had been dead for four days and it was half eaten. Like the back legs had been eaten away by the D-Con but the top half was still full and was kind of stuck in the gunk. Right? That was the place where my father needed to get to. No hesitation at all. Flashlight. Finds the compressor, the rat is on the floor,

Ranking the Hits

Billboard magazine publishes weekly charts of the most popular songs and albums. Modern technology makes it possible to count every time a song is played on the radio or television. Airplay and sales are tallied for more than a million songs every year. Hot 100 chart for pop songs, and *Billboard* 200 chart for albums.

under the compressor, hands me the flashlight and with his bare hands grabs the rat, snatches it from out of the gunk, tosses it to one side, and lays his bald head in the spot where that rat was. From that moment in my life, I decided I would never, ever complain about what I have to do for a living."[10]

In his spare time, Will was always listening to music. But the music world was changing. When Will was eleven, he heard a new song that left him amazed—"Rapper's Delight," performed by Sugarhill Gang, a trio from New York City. It was one of the first rap songs to be a commercial success.

The song was not a big hit in terms of sales. It reached only as high as number 36 on *Billboard* magazine's national Hot 100 chart.[11] Still, both in dance clubs and on radio stations across the country, "Rapper's Delight" was played often and regarded as a hit.

While some rap music focuses on social issues such as racial injustice or poverty, "Rapper's Delight" was a party rap song. The lyrics were funny, even silly. It was good-time music.

Will thought about Sugarhill Gang and decided they were not doing anything that he could not do. After all, he loved music and enjoyed writing poetry. All those Dr. Seuss books his mother used to read to him had left an impression. To Will's thinking, the rhythm and rhyme created by Dr. Seuss "sound a lot like hip-hop."[12] "I started rapping just as soon as I heard that first song," he said. "I rapped all day long, until I thought my mom was going to lose her mind! Music, after all, has always been in my heart. At first, I did it as a hobby, and I enjoyed it and got really good at it."[13]

The best places to check out rap artists at the time were inner-city street corners. Amateur rappers would challenge each other to impromptu rap contests. Will was always ready to jump right in. But some of the urban neighborhoods where rappers did their thing were rampant with drugs and crime.

Will spent many evenings in tough, dangerous neighborhoods, and his father did not want him getting into trouble. One day Will Sr. gave his son a memorable lesson. He told Will to hop into the car. Then he drove through one of the worst neighborhoods in Philadelphia. Will later said, "He pointed to the bums sleeping in the doorways and said, 'This is what people look like when they do drugs.'"[14] His father's antidrug message was clear.

Street corners were not the only places for novice rappers to make noise. At neighborhood block parties held in the streets, the music was provided by area disc jockeys, or deejays (DJs). At that time, recorded music was played on vinyl records. At the parties, the DJ supplying the music would stand behind a record player's turntable, often called a "wheel of steel," and scratch the needle (a small, pointed stylus) moving along the grooves of the record. Scratching some records and including snippets of others created a basic beat. The magic that rap DJs could produce with a turntable itself became an art form. The ones who worked the magic became known by a special name: turntablists.

Rappers at the parties would come onstage and recite original verses to the beat, creating informal competitions. Even though he was only twelve, Will earned respect from fellow rappers. Not lacking in confidence, Will boasted, "My reputation came from beating other rappers in street challenges. I never lost a street battle."[15]

Will began to see rap as more than a hobby. He said, "I was going to all those block parties, having fun and competing with my raps. It suddenly occurred to me, 'okay, if I'm going to party, I might as well get paid for it.'"[16]

Will was just in seventh grade when he started earning money as a rap disc jockey at parties. Within a few months, he was writing his own lyrics and rapping, as well as running the wheels of steel. Before long, Will had gained a reputation as one of southwest Philadelphia's red hot rappers.

Some of Will's early rap lyrics included profanity. One day his grandmother came across a page of lyrics he had written. After reading them, she wrote across the page, "Dear Willard, intelligent people do not use these words to express themselves."[17] Will took her scolding to heart and vowed never again to use swear words in his lyrics. "I knew I wanted my grandmother's approval," he later explained, "just as I wanted my parents' approval."[18]

Rap music was really catching fire, and Will's DJ jobs were keeping him busy. At home, however, there were major changes in the Smith family. Will was thirteen when his parents announced that they were divorcing. Will understood that no matter what was happening, his parents loved their children and wanted the best for them.[19] Will went to live with his mother, although he continued to stay close to his father. During his early teens, he often spent his after-school hours helping his father at work.

When he was fourteen and had finished eighth grade, Will graduated from Our Lady of Lourdes school. He entered ninth grade at a public school, Overbrook High. Unlike the students at Our Lady of Lourdes, Overbrook's student body was mostly African-American. Thanks to his charm and his willingness to play the class clown, Will had no trouble making new friends. He paid enough attention to his studies to get good but not great grades. Math and science were still the subjects he found easiest, though he also did well in English. He was still writing poetry and took a special liking to the works of Edgar Allan Poe. Outside school, Will continued to entertain friends with his creative turns at rap music.

Will teamed up with a school friend, Clarence Holmes, and they performed as a rap duo at local functions. Clarence, known by the nickname Clate, chose the rap name Ready Rock-C. Will did the writing and the rapping, and Clate created rhythmic sound effects. The two thought they were as good as the rap artists they heard on the radio, so one day they paid a visit to the Philadelphia-based rap record company Word Up.

The music business is tough. Every day, record producers encounter inexperienced garage bands and street rappers who are not nearly as good as they think they are. Will and Clate were the exceptions. Word Up's owner and producer, Dana Goodman, agreed that the duo had talent. They just did not have enough songs. Goodman sent them away but encouraged them to come back when they had more material.

That was the boost Will needed. He put his energies into writing music and making demonstration, or demo, tapes to bring to Word Up. But there are just twenty-four hours in a day, and Will was having trouble juggling both music and school. When one of Will's teachers told his mother that Will's grades were just barely good enough to get into college, his parents laid down the law: Rap was a fine hobby for weekends, but school was his first priority. They wanted him to be well rested every morning to face the school day.

Will did not always do what his parents wished. One evening, Will Sr. informed his son that his help would be needed the next morning. Will would have to be awake and alert at six A.M. Disregarding his dad, Will Jr. spent the night working at a gig and arrived home just fifteen minutes before he was supposed to be ready to go to work.

Will's father took him to the job site as scheduled. In the flooded basement of a delicatessen, Will was responsible for holding a flashlight so his father could see. Will's father was working with electrical wires, so being able to see clearly was a safety issue, too.

Suddenly Will was jolted by a piercing scream. He had fallen asleep and dropped the flashlight. The next thing he saw was his father's hair standing on end and smoke coming from his fingertips. His father's immediate reaction was to punch his son in the chest. Will said he felt that punch every day for the next ten years. After that frightening mishap, he stopped staying out so late and paid more attention to his schoolwork and getting enough sleep.

Will's teachers were not as tough as his father. On occasions when Will missed a homework assignment or did poorly on a test, his knack for creativity often saved him from punishment. Will came up with excuses that were original and funny, and he could charm his way out of a bad situation. In fact, Will was so good at it that the teachers at Overbrook High gave him a nickname: Prince Charming.

Soon Prince Charming would meet a jazzy DJ, and his life would change forever.

Chapter 3

HE'S THE DJ, I'M THE RAPPER

One day in January 1984, Will went to a neighborhood block party. The DJ working the turntable was seventeen-year-old Jeff Townes. Although Jeff had grown up near Will, the two had never met before.

Townes had earned a reputation as one of the best DJs in Philadelphia. He had set up a studio of sorts in his parents' basement. There he spent his leisure time experimenting with his portable four-track recorders. He tried a variety of different ideas, such as scratching two records at the same time and back spinning.

After working for a while as a DJ doing party gigs, Townes took a job at a local rap radio station. Jeff did not grow up listening to funk as Will had. Jeff's parents loved jazz, and as a kid Jeff had spent many hours listening to his parents' records. He took a liking to the music and even tried mixing jazz and rap. That led to Jeff's nickname: DJ Jazzy Jeff.

Jeff had teamed up with other rappers before, but they never seemed to click. So he did not expect much when at that January party Will came over to the turntable and asked Jeff if he would rap with him for a while.

The result was magic. Jeff later said that the two seemed to flow together as they played off each other's rhythms. After that, Will and Jeff got together a few more times. They rapped in Jeff's basement studio and put tracks together. Still, after his bad past experiences with other rappers, Jeff was hesitant to team up with another partner.

That attitude changed a few weeks later when the two bonded over a favorite amusement of teenage boys: gross-out humor. They were working a party. Jeff had taken along a spray can that appeared to be an air freshener. But it was really a gag spray can that emitted a foul smell when the nozzle was pushed. Jeff sprayed it at the party, and he and Will cracked up laughing. Jeff later said that the two of them just clicked. They had the same style of humor.

Will and Jeff began to spend more and more time writing and recording rap songs based on their life experiences. Since neither of them had grown up on the dangerous streets of a poor neighborhood, their subject matter was different from that of many rap artists. Their style was more like that of Sugarhill Gang. Instead of focusing on drugs and crime, Will and Jeff rapped about the ups and downs of ordinary teen life—issues like dating, going to the movies, and dealing with lame parents.

If the two were to work together as rappers, they needed to have a catchy name. Jeff was fine as DJ Jazzy Jeff, but Will wanted something edgier than Prince Charming. So he dropped Charming and replaced it with a slang word that was popular in the world of rap: *fresh*. According to Will: "At the time the word Fresh was *the* word. It was street talk for cool, the best."[1]

So Jeff and Will became DJ Jazzy Jeff and the Fresh Prince. They invited Will's first rap partner, Clate Holmes, to join them as the human beat box, just as he had done with Will.

In September 1984, Will began his junior year at Overbrook. Academically, he managed to maintain adequate grades. Socially, he continued to play the role of the goofy but charming kid. Years later, he said: "I think the popular terminology for what I was in high school was DORK."[2]

In his last two years of high school, Will made money working at parties with Townes. Will and Jeff, along with Clarence, also spent many hours in Jeff's recording studio, making demo tapes. When they felt they had created enough, they once again went to see Dana Goodman at Word Up. This time, the record producer was convinced that he had a winner and signed them almost immediately to a recording contract.

Will, now a high school senior, was about to become a professional music artist—but there was one big problem. His parents had always dreamed that he would go to college.

Though they were no longer married, Willard Sr. and Caroline shared the same goal of a top-notch education for their son. The computer industry was young and booming in the mid-1980s, and Will's father believed his son could be a successful computer engineer. With his parents' urging, Will took the Scholastic Aptitude Tests (SATs), which many colleges use as part of their admissions criteria. Even though his grades had dropped somewhat, Will's scores on the SATs were excellent.

Willard Sr. and Caroline urged their son to apply to some colleges. Will did so and was accepted right away at the Milwaukee School of Engineering. Then two recruiters from the Massachusetts Institute of Technology (MIT) interviewed Will. They tried to interest him in applying for MIT's two-year pre-engineering prep course. MIT is one of the best technology colleges in the United States. MIT students are among the brightest in the country. Attending MIT would be a major opportunity for Will if he had any interest in a career in computer engineering.

But that is not what Will wanted. He told his parents that he planned to become a rapper. His mother was outraged—and worried. Music, like all the arts, is a very competitive business. There are always more musicians trying to make it big than there are opportunities.

Will was able to work out a compromise with his parents. He asked them to consider his love for music, along with the fact that he was starting to have some success. They agreed to give him a year to work on his rap career. If it did not take off by the time the year was up, Will would go to college.

Will did not have to wait long to see results. Just a few weeks before Will graduated from high school, he and Jeff released a record on the Word Up label. It was a single, "Girls Ain't Nothing But Trouble."

The song was pure party rap. The rappers had fun exploring the problems involved in teenaged dating life and then putting them to music.

"Girls Ain't Nothing But Trouble" was first played on Philadelphia-area radio stations. Then radio stations elsewhere in the United States picked it up. Before long, the song crossed the Atlantic Ocean and could be heard on radio stations in England. Teenage boys understood the problems Will sang about, and even teenage girls could have a good laugh. Kids did not need to be African-American to relate to the lyrics. Perhaps that fact, along with the catchy backbeat, is what made the song popular. While it was not a monster hit, it made the top-twenty hit list in England and sold more than one hundred thousand copies worldwide.[3]

That summer, the rapper and the DJ went on their first concert tour, playing in cities across the United States and England. When their plane landed at Heathrow Airport in London, Will and Jeff noticed masses of cheering teenage girls. At first they did not realize the girls had come to see them. Will said, "There were screaming girls at the airport, and we thought, 'What is this? What are they screaming for?'"[4]

Still, not everybody loved their record. It might seem that a song as lighthearted as "Girls Ain't Nothing But Trouble" would be unlikely to ignite controversy. That is especially true considering the severe lyrics of much hard-edged gangsta rap. But no work of art, whether a song, a stage play, a movie, or a painting, is universally admired by everyone.

The criticism of "Girls Ain't Nothing But Trouble" fell into two different categories. On the one hand, some journalists and feminists knocked the song for being sexist. Will blasted those critics for reading into the song a message that did not exist. He said that he always had the utmost respect for the women in his family and would never write a song demeaning women. He insisted that it was just a fun song about the misunderstandings boys and girls have about dating.[5]

The other criticism came mainly from the African-American community, especially fellow rap artists. To them, DJ Jazzy Jeff and the Fresh Prince's rap music was lightweight. They faulted the duo for not representing the black experience. "Girls Ain't Nothing But Trouble" was not the angry music of rap artists such as N.W.A and Public Enemy. Other rappers pointed to the fact that "Girls Ain't Nothing But Trouble" was one of the first rap records bought in large volume by young white people. Will and Jeff were accused of selling out their black heritage by softening the soul of gritty, urban rap music to suit suburban white teenagers.

This criticism from his fellow rappers was tougher for Will to take than the charge of sexism. To be accused of betraying his heritage was a personal insult. Will said these critics were stereotyping African Americans. What about the many African Americans who live in comfortable homes with stable families? Does not living in crime-ridden neighborhoods make these people less black? Will and Jeff's goal was to broaden rap's appeal. "We want to bring rap out of the ghetto," Will said.[6]

Some years later, Smith explained why he felt it necessary to keep profanity and mean-spiritedness out of his music: "Rap music—people can act like it's not—but rap music is for kids. You know it's completely directed at children and impressionable minds and I just think it's dangerous to pump that kind of cavalier misogyny [hatred of women] and hatred in young minds."[7] Even though some critics had accused "Girls Ain't Nothing But Trouble" of being sexist, the song was very mild compared with some hard-edged rap that truly degraded women.

Will and Jeff were not the first musical artists to broaden the appeal of rap. In 1986, a New York rap trio called Run-D.M.C. had teamed up with two white musicians from the rock band Aerosmith—lead singer Steve Tyler and lead guitarist Joe Perry—to record a rap version of Aerosmith's hit "Walk This Way." The song was a big hit and reached number four on *Billboard* magazine's national Hot 100 chart.[8]

By now, DJ Jazzy Jeff and the Fresh Prince had taped plenty of songs that they were aching to release. The next logical step was to put out an album. The success of their hit single drew attention from record companies bigger than the Philadelphia-based Word Up. These companies had bigger networks and could distribute records to more music stores than Word Up. So Smith and Townes left Word Up and signed with Jive Records.

Run-D.M.C.

Run-D.M.C. was the first rap group to achieve mainstream success. The three members, Run (Joseph Simmons), D.M.C. (Darryl McDaniels), and Jam Master Jay (Jason Mizell), all grew up in a middle-class neighborhood in the New York City borough of Queens. Run and D.M.C. met while rapping at a local club for teenagers. They stayed in touch while attending different colleges and later asked another friend, deejay Jam Master Jay, to join their act. Their first single, "It's Like That," was released in 1983, and they had several more hits in the 1980s. Run's brother, Russell Simmons, is a famous rap music producer.

Dana Goodman was not pleased to see them go; after all, he was the one who had given them their first break. However, Smith and Townes wanted to reach a bigger audience and achieve a higher level of success, and they believed they had to move on.[9]

They again teamed up with their human beat box, Clate Holmes, or Ready Rock-C. In 1987 the trio released *Rock the House*, an album named after one of its songs. "Rock the House" was written by Clate Holmes. The songs on *Rock the House* are similar in style to "Girls Ain't Nothing But Trouble," which is also included on the album. They are light and humorous and touch on topics that all teenagers can understand, regardless of their race or religion or whether they are rich or poor.

Will and Jeff's songs on *Rock the House* differed from those of hard-edged rappers in another notable way. Gangsta rappers often brag about themselves, rapping about their success with women. In his songs, Will often made himself the butt of the joke.

One of the songs on *Rock the House*, "Guys Ain't Nothing But Trouble," was performed by a female rapper. Will said they included it for fun, but some critics believed it was meant as an answer to the charges of sexism. Another number, "Just One of Those Days," talks about getting in trouble at school and about car problems. "Just Rockin'" is about a teenager who plays his sound system so loud that the neighbors complain to his parents. The album's title song, "Rock the House," is about entertaining at a party. In some of the songs, the rappers thank Dana Goodman for giving them their first break.

Going for the Gold

A Gold Record is awarded when the sales of individual singles or albums hit five hundred thousand. A Platinum Record means that sales have reached one million. A Diamond Record is given in recognition of selling 10 million copies.

Rock the House sold six hundred thousand copies, a hit by any standards.[10] The high sales netted the rappers their first Gold Record. For Will, that put an end to the question of going to college: He was on the road to stardom. Although his parents were disappointed, they were now ready to let Will follow his dreams. If he was to have any further education, it would be in the rough world of show business.

Smith and Townes got busy on a second album. Rap music might seem easy to write, because it uses borrowed beats and what appears to be simple poetry. But writing rap is harder than people might expect. Townes once described the process: "The hardest part of making records is always coming up with a concept, and we would sit in a room for days just wondering what we were going to talk about and trying to come up with something. But once we came up with a topic, then the rest of the song would come within about fifteen or twenty minutes. We would bounce ideas off each other. I would pretty much do the music and we would lay the rap over the top of it. And then he would kind of tweak it."[11]

DJ Jazzy Jeff and the Fresh Prince's next album came out in 1988. It was the album *He's the DJ, I'm the Rapper*, with the song "Parents Just Don't Understand," which earned them their first Grammy. The record is more technologically advanced and musically creative than *Rock the House*, but the subject matter is similar. In "Parents Just Don't Understand," Will sings about how embarrassing it is to shop with one's parents, and how he got in trouble for taking his parents' car without their permission. The song "Nightmare on My

Street" pays tribute to Jeff's favorite horror movie series, *Nightmare on Elm Street*. Both songs were released as singles in 1988. "Parents Just Don't Understand" reached number 12 on *Billboard* magazine's Top 100 list, and "Nightmare on My Street" got as high as number 15 that summer.[12]

He's the DJ, I'm the Rapper surpassed *Rock the House*, selling more than 3 million copies.[13] Smith and Townes, with their first Platinum Record, were rich. They were also creative businessmen, starting their own 900 telephone line. Fans paid roughly $2.45 to call the 900 number and hear the taped voices of Jazzy Jeff and the Fresh Prince. The duo would discuss subjects such as plans for new records, upcoming concert dates, and maybe some personal gossip.[14]

In 1989 they released their third album, *And in This Corner . . .* , featuring the party rap that DJ Jazzy Jeff and Fresh Prince had become known for. The most-played cut from the album was "I Think I Can Beat Mike Tyson," a fantasy in which Will takes on Tyson, who was the world heavyweight boxing champion. Of course, Will loses the match as soon as Tyson hits him with his first punch.

In early 1989 Will Smith was twenty years old. But unlike most twenty-year-olds, Smith was a millionaire. The rappers' 900 telephone line alone brought in over $10 million.[15] Record sales only added to his wealth.

Unlike many millionaires, who work for years to earn their fortune, Smith and Townes had earned theirs in a very short time. They were young and immature and had no savings plans for their money. Almost as quickly as Smith earned his millions, he spent it all.

Smith bought a mansion outside Philadelphia. The home had five bedrooms, a pool room, and a living room, where he installed a basketball net. Sometimes he paid for travel expenses for his parents to join him while on tour. When he was bored, he went shopping. On two occasions he flew to London and Tokyo just to buy clothes. He also purchased all kinds of fancy jewelry, including a gold necklace that spelled out "Fresh Prince" in diamonds.

Before long, Smith was the owner of six cars and two motorcycles. His father thought Will was wasting his money. He once barked at his son, "Why do you need six cars when you only have one butt?"[16] Meanwhile, Smith was busy using his new wealth to impress women and throw parties for his friends—and with so much money, he suddenly had a lot of friends.

The rap duo's third album, *And in This Corner . . .* , sold well, but not nearly as well as *He's the DJ, I'm the Rapper*. About five hundred thousand copies were sold, earning the album a Gold Record.[17] For most people, this would have provided more than enough money, but it was not enough for Will to keep up his extravagant lifestyle.

Before long, Will received word from the Internal Revenue Service (IRS), the department of the United States government that collects income taxes. The IRS notified Smith that he owed the government millions of dollars in taxes. But the rap artist had one big problem. He had not put any money aside for taxes.

Being famous did not earn Smith any special favors with the IRS. All United States citizens, even superstars, are required to pay their taxes. Smith used the money he had left to pay some of his tax bills. Yet he still owed more. Suddenly, the high-living Fresh Prince was broke. "It was weird," he said, "because I had six cars and couldn't buy gas."[18]

Smith lost something else, too. Many of the friends who had gathered around him when he was rich abandoned him now that he was in debt. This humbling experience provided an important lesson for the young man from Philadelphia.

Chapter 4

FROM RAPPER TO ACTOR

Will Smith had bills to pay, and he needed to make more money. What if his career as a rapper did not last? He decided to pursue another potentially high-paying career path: acting. Philadelphia was a fine city for a young rap musician, but he did not consider it the best place for someone who wanted to be a professional actor. So Smith began to think about moving west, to Los Angeles. His partner Jeff, on the other hand, wanted to stay in Philadelphia, where his family and friends lived.

Smith had an advantage over many people who want to get into acting: He was already well known. In fact, he and Jeff had been considered for the lead roles in *House Party*, a movie about two teenage rappers who throw a party for their friends while their parents are out of town. The soundtrack for *House Party* is filled with rap music and dancing. After seriously considering the offer, Smith and Townes turned it down. Smith wanted his first acting role to be a more serious one. He also wanted to prove that he was versatile and that he did not have to be cast as a party rapper.

The rap duo Kid'n Play starred in *House Party*, which turned out to be a huge hit with moviegoers when it opened in 1990. It seemed that Smith had missed out on a wonderful opportunity. Still, something even better was waiting for him just around the corner.

At that time, the African-American comedian Arsenio Hall was the host of a nighttime talk show. One night Hall devoted his program to the life and career of Quincy Jones, the multitalented musician, composer, and record producer. While Smith was not asked to appear on the air, he was invited to join the cast and crew at a party celebrating Jones backstage.

Smith saw this celebration as more than a chance to party. It was a great opportunity to network—that is, to meet others in the field who might help with his career. For Smith, this networking paid off big time. One of the party guests was record executive Benny Medina.

Medina had an idea for a television show based on his life. Medina's father had walked out on his family when Benny was very small. Tragedy struck when Benny's mother died suddenly. There were no relatives to care for Benny, so he was placed in various foster homes over the years.

Quincy Jones

Quincy Jones started out as a musician, but he has since become best known as one of the greatest record producers in the music industry. Born in 1933, Jones first achieved success as a jazz trumpet player in the 1950s. His first stint as a record producer came in Paris, France, in 1957, and in 1961 he became the first African-American vice president of a major record label, Mercury Records. He has since written musical scores for many movies and television programs and has produced all types of recordings.

By 2011, Jones had won twenty-seven Grammy awards.

When he was about fifteen, a white composer named Jack Elliot adopted Benny. Elliot is a wealthy man whose friends include some of the biggest names in the music business. He and his wife and three children had a home in the wealthy southern California city of Beverly Hills.

The Elliots converted one of their garages into a bedroom for Benny. He went to Beverly Hills High School along with the children of celebrities and other show business figures. Suddenly, the poor orphan from one of the poorest neighborhoods in southern California was living in one of the area's richest communities.

Young Benny knew he was lucky to have such a golden opportunity. He took advantage of it by getting a job in the music industry. He worked hard and over time became a record company executive: the vice president in charge of the black music division of Warner Brothers records.

Medina thought his life story would make a good television situation comedy. It would be based on a common theme in comedy: the fish out of water. The main character would be trying to adapt not only to a new family but also to a different way of life. At the party for Quincy Jones, Medina told Smith about his idea, and Smith made it clear that he would be very interested in acting in such a comedy. The two parted, but Medina told Smith he would keep in touch.

At first glance, it might seem that Smith and Medina had little in common. Smith was from the East Coast; Medina had been born and raised in Los Angeles. While Smith grew up in a comfortable neighborhood, Medina came out of one of the poorest and toughest neighborhoods in Los Angeles. It is an area called Watts, where drugs and gang violence are part of daily life.

Medina went through many steps to make his idea come true. First, he had to find a producer—someone to supervise and provide the money—for his television program. Medina knew just the person to speak to. He approached Quincy Jones, who knew all sorts of important people in the entertainment business. First, Medina had to convince Jones that his idea was a good one.

That was not a problem. Jones liked the concept and thought Smith would be perfect for the role. As Jones and Medina spoke, they decided to twist the premise of the proposed show. Instead of a wealthy white family, they decided to feature a well-to-do African-American one. Medina recalled a rich African-American family who lived near the Elliots in Beverly Hills. He said, "There was no relationship between what *I* considered to be the black experience and what *they* considered the black experience in America. It was like two completely different cultures."[1]

It was also decided that Smith's character would be a relative, rather than a foster child. He would play a cousin from Philadelphia on the verge of getting into trouble. He would be shuttled off to live with a wealthy and successful branch of the family in the hopes that their good influence would rub off on the troubled teen and straighten him out.

Jones knew that the NBC television network was looking for a family-oriented comedy to put on its Monday night schedule. For Jones and Medina, the next step was to take their idea to NBC, where they met with two executives, Brandon Tartikoff and Warren Littlefield. Jones and Medina had to convince Tartikoff and Littlefield that their program would attract many viewers. The meeting was a success: Tartikoff and Littlefield loved the idea.

At the time, Smith and Townes were traveling around the country on a concert tour. It was at a concert performance in 1989 that Smith met someone special. The setting was San Diego State University in California, and a young woman in the audience caught Smith's eye. After Smith and Townes's set was finished, Will approached her. Tanya Moore was a senior majoring in business at the university. Though they had just met, he told her she was the girl of his dreams. They began dating, and Smith was delighted with how well they got along. "What's good about Tanya," said Smith, "is that she thinks like a guy, so I don't miss my buddies. It's like, I can't relate to somebody crying because she broke a fingernail."[2]

Meanwhile, Jones and Medina were trying to persuade NBC that Will Smith was the right person for their new show. That was not so easy. The final say would be in the hands of Tartikoff, who was the head of NBC's entertainment division. After viewing some of Smith's music videos, Tartikoff was not convinced.

Sure, Smith was charming and funny in the music videos. But there was no scripted dialogue as there would be in a television show. In the videos, Smith was himself. He was not playing a different character or reacting to another actor's dialogue. In the proposed show, Smith would be the lead actor. It would be up to him to carry the program. That was a lot of responsibility, and Tartikoff did not want to take a big chance on an untested actor.

Jones and Medina would not quit. They insisted that Smith was perfect for the role, and Tartikoff finally compromised. He said he would consider Smith as long as he passed an audition. Medina tracked down Smith on tour in Indiana. This was the chance Smith had been waiting for. He packed his bags, took a break from the tour, and flew the next day to Los Angeles for the audition.

On a winter day early in 1990, Quincy Jones, Benny Medina, Will Smith, and NBC executive Warren Littlefield met inside Jones's mansion in the well-to-do Los Angeles neighborhood of Bel-Air. Smith was given a script and sent to a spare bedroom to rehearse. A little while later, Will came out of the bedroom, nervous but ready to perform. He put his heart into the audition and gave it his best shot.

Littlefield recognized that Smith seemed anxious but was amazed by his performance. "There were beads of sweat [on Smith's face]," he said. "But Will read from a script and just nailed it. I sat there thinking, 'Whoa! Just bottle this guy!'"[3]

Smith was hired right away. He went back to Philadelphia to pack up the rest of his belongings. It was not easy to say good-bye to family and friends. Still, there would be another advantage to living in Los Angeles. He would be closer to his girlfriend, Tanya Moore, who had by now graduated from college. After Smith settled into an apartment near the NBC studios, Tanya left San Diego and moved in with him.

In a way, Smith would be playing himself in the new show. His character was even named Will Smith. Soon, the rest of the cast was hired. James Avery, a veteran actor of television and movies, was cast as Will's uncle, Judge Philip Banks. An actress with experience on Broadway and in movies, Janet Hubert-Whitten, was chosen to play Uncle Phil's wife, Aunt Vivian.

The Banks children, Will's first cousins in the show, included a spoiled teenage girl named Hilary, played by Karyn Parsons; a conservative and proper teenage boy named Carlton, played by Alfonso Ribeiro; and twelve-year-old Ashley, played by Tatyana M. Ali. The Banks family lived in a fancy mansion with a swimming pool and tennis courts. The Bankses even had their own butler, Geoffrey, who was also African-American, played by the British actor Joseph Marcell.

Two principal scriptwriters, Andy and Susan Borowitz, were hired to create the episodes. The Borowitzes had written for several television shows. Their biggest success was *Family Ties*, the 1980s situation comedy that had made Michael J. Fox a star. The Borowitzes, who knew little about rap music, had to give themselves a quick education. Susan Borowitz said, "I listened to rap for the first time because I had to, like a homework assignment. I found that the music told stories and had really clever rhymes . . . far more literate than rock & roll. It opened my eyes."[4]

The show now had writers and a cast, but there was no guarantee it would make it on the air. First, they had to tape a sample episode, known in the television business as a pilot. It would be shown to a test audience to see their reaction. The test audience loved the pilot, and *The Fresh Prince of Bel-Air* was given a go-ahead. The show premiered on NBC on September 10, 1990.

Most of the reviews at the time said the show was good but not great. *The Boston Globe* rated the premiere episode three stars out of four, but added, "Like the best of the new comedies, 'Fresh Prince' isn't anything to get excited about, but . . . it has enough good moments to warrant future attention."[5] A *New York Times* critic was taken with Smith's talent, writing that Smith displayed "a strong sense of comedic timing" and praised him for his ability to ad-lib. The critic also noted that "on the few occasions he muffed a line, [Smith] calmly called out, 'Sorry, Mom,' to his mother, visiting from Philadelphia and watching the performance from the audience."[6]

Not all the reviewers were as kind. Another *New York Times* critic expressed concern that the Fresh Prince was too much of a "smart aleck" and added, "Making matters shakier, the brightly, energetic Mr. Smith seems to be learning how to act on the job and is frequently overshadowed by the rest of the cast, particularly James Avery as the father and Karyn Parsons as the older daughter, Hilary."[7]

Smith also had to deal with one other tough critic: himself. He was so nervous about forgetting his lines that he would memorize entire scripts. Then he would say the other actors' lines to himself as they were speaking them. In some of the earliest episodes, Smith can be seen mouthing the lines on camera.

Although most television viewers did not even notice, his costars did, and it bothered them. Smith later said, "When I watch those episodes, it's disgusting. My performances were terrible."[8] Smith humbly admitted that what saved him and the show were the performances of his more established costars.

Although he was three thousand miles away in Philadelphia, Smith's friend and partner Jeff Townes flew to Los Angeles for a guest appearance on the show. Townes made his debut in the second episode as Will's best friend, Jazz, and continued to play Jazz off and on for four years. While some episodes of *The Fresh Prince of Bel-Air* focused on the conflict of a street kid trying to fit into a wealthy and refined family, others directly confronted African-American issues. In one episode, Carlton wants to prove that he is just as black in spirit as his cousin, so Will forces him to survive in a tough Los Angeles neighborhood for two days. In another, Will and Carlton are stopped by police while driving an expensive car. They are arrested for car theft because the police do not believe these two young African-American men could legally be driving such a costly car. That story line came right out of Smith's real life. Even after he had made his first millions, he was stopped on many occasions by police who were suspicious seeing a person of his race and age behind the wheel of a luxury car.

One particular episode focuses on Uncle Phil's background. When Phil's parents visit from their home in a backwoods part of North Carolina, they embarrass the dignified judge with a story about the pet pig he owned as a child. The point of the episode was that even though Uncle Phil was now wealthy, he still had plenty to tell Will about growing up poor and black.

As with Smith's music career, *The Fresh Prince of Bel-Air* had its share of critics from the rap community. Fab 5 Freddy, a rapper who hosted a television program titled *Yo! MTV Raps*, was especially tough on Smith and *The Fresh Prince* for not realistically representing the black experience.

In response, Smith praised the diversity of the African-American characters on his show: "There are different types of Black people. And everyone is represented on the show. We're showing something that's never been shown on television. We're showing Black-on-Black prejudice. It's more of a class thing. My aunt represents the middle. Her husband is snooty and a Black Republican."[9]

Smith was careful not to put down the specific rap artists who criticized him. He said, "I have a lot of opinions. I agree with things that Chuck D and Public Enemy say, but I have a different way of expressing myself. I like blending a message with comedy so it's subtle."[10]

On the other hand, there were times when Smith became very defensive. He told one reporter, "There is a problem in the black community now with equating stupid with cool and smart with corny. And for me there is a certain aggressiveness to my intelligence that I like to keep intact. And those big hardcore guys think you're tough because you're not smart. Well, let's fight if you're so tough. Let's see who's the toughest. Let's see if your stupidity is tougher than my intelligence."[11]

The Fresh Prince of Bel-Air had satisfactory but not fantastic ratings throughout the 1990–1991 season. Still, it was renewed for a second year. More episodes would be created, and bigger things would be in store for both Smith and the show.

Chapter 5

Six Degrees of the Fresh Prince

While Smith was successfully starring in a television program, he did not want to give up recording. The two careers kept him busy, but he felt he could handle it. "I'm doing the show from nine to five," he said. "And from six until midnight I'm in the studio working on an album. As long as I get my eight hours of sleep, I'm fine."[1]

Some successful people Smith's age get caught up in the Los Angeles party scene and find themselves in trouble with money, drugs, alcohol, or personal relationships. Smith had already been caught up in a high-spending glamorous life and learned a lesson. He did not want to repeat his mistakes of two years earlier, when he lost all his money. He was ready to put all his energy into his career. "I don't need a social life," he said in 1990. "You see, I've got to work now and I'll have a social life when I'm thirty. My mother is going to fly out here to keep things in line. See, I'm not into the L.A. lifestyle, the clubs, etc. It takes your mind off work."[2]

Homebase, the album Smith was working on during those long hours, was released in 1991. As usual, he recorded it with DJ Jazzy Jeff. A single from *Homebase*, titled "Summertime," became a big hit, reaching number four on the *Billboard* national song chart and selling more than a million copies.[3] Like Will and Jeff's other songs, "Summertime" was a lighthearted look at teenage life. Some critics found it to be a more sophisticated record than some of the duo's earlier works. In "Summertime," the Fresh Prince rapped about looking for girls, cruising in his car, having fun at an outdoor barbecue, and shooting baskets on a local court. A well-known Philadelphia-based turntablist and hip-hop producer, King Britt, said, "That was a monumental song in hip-hop. It was a clear picture of what summer is for the black community."[4]

"Summertime" earned the duo its second Grammy award, as best rap song. It also earned another honor: an Image Award from the NAACP (National Association for the Advancement of Colored People), one of the nation's oldest and most respected civil rights organizations. NAACP Image Awards are given annually to those whose work represents positive aspects of African-American life. It was the first of several Smith would receive.

Meanwhile, the album *Homebase* was a huge hit as well, selling about 1.2 million copies.[5] The exposure Smith received by being on television every week likely helped boost sales.

Always ambitious, Smith began to consider how to break into movies. His first movie role was in *Where the Day Takes You*, a drama about the hard lives of teenage runaways living on the streets of Los Angeles. Smith plays Manny, a runaway confined to a wheelchair. He decided to take the part for two reasons. It showed that he could play someone other than the joke-cracking wise guy on *The Fresh Prince of Bel-Air*. Smith also liked knowing that moviegoers would see the dark plight of homeless teens. In one scene, a cruel thug tips Manny out of his wheelchair and beats him up. *Where the Day Takes You* was not filmed by one of the major movie studios, and it was not widely distributed to movie theaters across the country. As a result, not as many people saw it. However, many movie casting directors did see the movie and were impressed by Smith's performance. He started receiving offers to make bigger movies.

About this time, Smith and Tanya Moore broke up. It was not long before Smith began dating someone else. One day in 1991 Will was backstage at the taping of a television program called *A Different World*. The show was a spin-off— that is, a program featuring a character from another show. In this case, the lead character was Denise Huxtable, one of the daughters on *The Cosby Show*. Like *The Fresh Prince of Bel-Air*, the show *A Different World* had a mainly African-American cast.

The Cosby Show

The Cosby Show, a situation comedy that ran from 1984 to 1992, is viewed as one of the most successful television programs ever. The comedian Bill Cosby developed the show to present an African-American family that all television viewers—regardless of their race—could relate to. Cosby played a doctor who was married to an attorney. Their five children had the same problems that most kids go through, from writing book reports to sharing a room with a sibling. The Huxtable family was proud of its African-American heritage, which was celebrated in many episodes. *The Cosby Show* is still seen in reruns on television.

On the set of *A Different World* that day, Smith met a fashion design student named Sheree Zampino. He was immediately attracted to her, though apparently the feeling was not mutual. Smith asked Zampino out several times before she said yes. After their first date, the two were inseparable. Zampino enjoyed being with Smith and was taken by his sense of humor and charm.

The couple became engaged on Christmas Eve, 1991, and they were married on May 9, 1992, at a seaside hotel in Santa Barbara, California. With his tax debts to the government finally paid, Smith indulged his friends and family with a lavish wedding reception. Of course, Jeff Townes was in attendance, as were major celebrities, including the actor Denzel Washington and the basketball star Magic Johnson. *Ebony*, one of the best-known magazines geared toward African Americans, selected Will and Sheree as one of the year's ten hottest couples.

By the end of the year, the couple had become a trio. Sheree gave birth to a son, Willard Christopher Smith III, in December 1992. With son, father, and grandfather all having the same name, the Smiths decided to give the baby a nickname to avoid confusion. They call him Trey, a form of the word three, since he is the third Will Smith.

This was a promising time for Smith. Aside from embarking on a new marriage and becoming a father, he made plans to appear in two more movies. The first one was a science fiction movie to be titled *Biofeed*. The other was a baseball movie, *Scout*. Smith was excited about both films.

But not all movie ideas get made, and neither *Biofeed* nor *Scout* was ever filmed. Smith was offered a role in another movie, however, which turned out to be a smash hit. It was a comedy titled *Made in America*, and featured two big stars: Whoopi Goldberg and Ted Danson.

The plot is a clever one. Whoopi Goldberg plays a single mother whose daughter, played by Nia Long, is a high school senior. The daughter decides to go on a quest to find her natural father. Early in the movie, the girl learns that he is a white man, played by Danson. He is certainly not what she expected. To make matters worse, Danson's character, a used-car salesman, is a crude and obnoxious man who stars in embarrassing, goofy commercials on television. The movie combines slapstick humor and a serious look at race relations. *Made in America* was released in 1993.

In *Made in America*, Smith plays a supporting role as the daughter's boyfriend. Critics liked his performance, and this film exposed him to a larger audience than *Where the Day Takes You* had. In addition, Smith learned a lot from observing the acting veterans Goldberg and Danson.

Along with his growing success in movies and television, Smith was still making music. Later in 1993, he and Jeff Townes released their fifth album, *Code Red*, which contained a harder-edged rap than they had created in the past. One cut, "Boom! Shake the Room," reached number thirteen on the *Billboard* music charts.[6] Overall, however, *Code Red* had mediocre sales. Some critics believed that Smith was distracted by his movie and television roles and did not put as much effort into the album. Except for a greatest-hits collection released in 1998, *Code Red* was the last album the Fresh Prince and Jazzy Jeff did together.

Music aside, Smith's acting career was about to take off. For one thing, *The Fresh Prince of Bel-Air* was having a better year than its first. Over the course of the 1991–1992 television season, the show finished in the ratings as the twenty-second most watched program.[7]

Movie producers now considered Smith ready to take on his first costarring movie role. The part he selected was very unlike him, and some friends thought he was making a huge mistake. *Six Degrees of Separation* is based on a Broadway play, which itself is based loosely on a true story. As Paul, the lead character, Smith plays a young gay man. Paul is a con artist who charms his way into the lives of the Kittredges, a wealthy white couple in New York City. Paul claims to be the son of the famous actor Sidney Poitier. He also tells the Kittredges that he is acquainted with their children. In reality, he has never even met Poitier—to say nothing of being related to him—and does not know the Kittredges' children.

The movie explores a number of themes. One is that even intelligent people can be easily deceived. Another is homosexuality. A third is race relations. *Six Degrees of Separation* points out that some white people make automatic judgments about African Americans. Whites are often fearful of letting blacks into their homes, supposing they might be criminals. However, the Kittredges feel safe with Paul because he is clean-cut and well spoken. Yet despite his well-mannered appearance, he is a thief who takes advantage of them.

Unlike the madcap comedy of *The Fresh Prince of Bel-Air*, the movie *Six Degrees of Separation* is a drama. Reviewers paid special attention to Smith's choice of role. One movie critic, Ben Falk from the British Broadcasting Company (BBC), wrote, "Anyone who watched Will Smith's sitcom, *The Fresh Prince of Bel-Air*, would know he had a talent for comedy. Which is why it was strange that he decided to launch his big-screen acting career proper with *Six Degrees of Separation*—a literate, wordy and comparatively serious adaptation of a successful stage play."[8]

Falk continued, "But anyone who doubts him will soon be eating their words. Smith puts in a highly effective performance as Paul. . . . Smith is the revelation, belying his lightweight background to produce a character of immense depth, intelligence and heart."[9]

Falk's review was one of many positive ones that Smith received. Rita Kempley of *The Washington Post* said that Smith played the role of Paul "with cheek and charisma."[10] Still, not all critics were so praiseworthy. The respected movie reviewer Janet Maslin of *The New York Times* wrote, "Mr. Smith recites his lines plausibly without bringing great passion to the role."[11]

Fortunately for Smith, more critics agreed with Falk and Kempley than with Maslin. Smith's hard work had transformed him from a rapper into a polished actor. Yet Smith's rap background still influenced what he did and said—and one of his comments got him into a bit of trouble.

Male rap music artists have an image of toughness. Because of that image, Smith was not sure at first if he wanted to play a gay man in *Six Degrees of Separation*. The script called for Smith's character to kiss another man, something Smith refused to do. During interviews, Smith publicly discussed his hesitancy about the role. As a result, some gay rights activists accused him of being homophobic, or prejudiced against gays. Smith said he was not homophobic, but that not being gay made him play the role differently. Later, he admitted that he had been overly concerned with what his friends would think about him if he kissed a man on screen. He said, "It was immature on my part. . . . I wasn't emotionally stable enough to artistically commit to that aspect of the film."[12]

Meanwhile, Smith kept busy with *The Fresh Prince of Bel-Air*, which continued to do well. The news at the end of the 1992–1993 season was an addition to the cast. Aunt Vivian gives birth to the Banks family's fourth child, a son they name Nicholas but call Nicky. That season, *The Fresh Prince of Bel-Air* finished as the nation's sixteenth most watched television program.[13]

The next season, 1993–1994, brought further changes to the show. The producers wanted to keep *The Fresh Prince of Bel-Air* truly fresh in more ways than one. The characters of Will and Carlton graduate from high school and enroll in college at the fictional University of Los Angeles. Then Will's old girlfriend from Philadelphia moves to Los Angeles, bringing all sorts of complications into his world.

Behind the scenes there were more changes, some brought on by Smith himself. Andy and Susan Borowitz, who had begun as writers on the show, were now the executive producers. Smith believed the show's plots had become too filled with slapstick comedy and had stopped reflecting the African-American experience. Filled with confidence after his movie successes, Smith did not hesitate to approach the Borowitzes with his concerns. He wanted the show to be changed, he said.

However, the ratings were still high. Without high ratings, the show would likely be canceled and everyone involved with it, including the actors, would be out of work. The Borowitzes were hesitant to make any changes. They believed in the old saying, If it isn't broken, then don't fix it.

Smith was frustrated. At one point, he confided in one of his idols, the legendary actor and comedian Bill Cosby. He told Cosby that the writers were creating weak scripts. If he expected Cosby to immediately agree, Smith was disappointed. Smith said, "When I complained about the writing on the show, Bill suggested I write a script. 'Just write one and don't go to sleep until it's finished,' he told me."[14]

Taking Cosby's advice, Smith soon discovered that script writing is not easy. He also learned a hard lesson about judging other people's work. "When I met the writers the next day, I had a lot less anger and a lot more understanding of the process."[15]

Still, that did not change his mind about the show's direction, which he felt should better reflect the African-American experience. He got together with Benny Medina to discuss his concerns. After his experience trying to write a script, Smith knew that changing the show would not be easy, but he thought it was important.

Medina agreed with Smith and suggested a compromise solution to the problem between Smith and the Borowitzes. Smith would be allowed to offer the Borowitzes plot ideas before the scripts were written. Unhappy with the idea of an actor telling them what they should write, the Borowitzes promptly quit. An African-American producer named Winifred Hervey-Stallworth replaced them.

The show's tone changed almost immediately. For one thing, Will's character got a job and began acting more responsibly. There was still humor—after all, *The Fresh Prince of Bel-Air* was a comedy—but there was less emphasis on silly jokes and slapstick. Fortunately, these changes did not affect the show's ratings, which remained just as high as before.

While that problem was solved, the public soon learned that offscreen, the show's cast was not one big, happy family. Smith and Janet Hubert-Whitten, who played Aunt Viv, were not getting along. At the end of the third season, in the spring of 1993, Hubert-Witten's contract to act in the show was not renewed.

When people are in show business, their personal conflicts end up in the gossip columns. Reporters know that the public has an endless fascination with news about celebrities. Smith told reporters that Hubert-Whitten resented the fact that Smith, not she, was the star. Hubert-Whitten countered that Smith wanted her fired out of revenge. She said she sometimes reprimanded him for being rude, and this was his way of getting back at her. Their disagreements did not make either Hubert-Whitten or Smith look good in the public eye.[16]

When new episodes of *The Fresh Prince of Bel-Air* resumed on television in fall 1993, the character of Aunt Viv was played by a different actress: Daphne Maxwell Reid, who had appeared as a lead in a number of other TV series. This change in casting was barely addressed in the show. The only reference to it was a comment by Jeff Townes, playing Jazz. At one point, Jazz tells Aunt Viv that she sure has changed since she had the baby.

Philip and Viv's son Nicky made his first appearance at the beginning of the fourth season. In the world of television sitcoms, time does not move as it does in real life. Even though Nicky had been born in the spring of 1993, when the show started up again less than a year later, he was already five years old.

Audiences did not care that the baby seemed to have gone through a time machine. *The Fresh Prince of Bel-Air* finished the 1993–1994 season ranked as the twenty-first most watched program.[17] Even so, Smith knew that the show would not go on forever. He wanted something even bigger—a blockbuster movie hit.

Chapter 6

BAD BOYS AND ALIEN INVADERS

T he movie *Batman Forever* was being cast in 1994. The actor Val Kilmer had been signed to play Batman, but the role of his sidekick, Robin, was still open. Smith, who wanted to be in an action movie, would have loved to get the part. The trouble was that Smith was one of many actors who wanted to play Robin. The role went to character actor Chris O'Donnell, who had gotten rave reviews in 1993 for his supporting role in *Scent of a Woman*.

Smith has not always gotten the roles he wanted, but he does not attribute it to racism. Smith says, "The execs don't care about what color you are, they care about how much money you make. Hollywood is not really black or white—it's green. The real key is that the more black actors are successful at the box office, the more opportunities that is going to open up."[1]

Though he missed out on the role of Robin, another opportunity was just ahead. Two movie producers, Don Simpson and Jerry Bruckheimer, had wanted for some time to make a police action movie. *Bad Boys* was to be a combination comedy and drama starring the comedic actors Jon Lovitz and Dana Carvey.

When plans to hire Lovitz and Carvey did not work out, Simpson and Bruckheimer tapped the comedian Martin Lawrence for one of the parts. Smith strongly hoped to get the other lead role in *Bad Boys*. For one thing, he was familiar with Lawrence's work and liked the idea of being in a movie with him. He also thought being in an action comedy would be challenging as well as fun. Finally, if the movie was a success, it would give Smith's career a huge boost. True, he had done a good job in *Six Degrees of Separation*. But that was a quirky character study, the type of movie that does not draw a huge audience. The movies that attract the most viewers tend to be well-made action films.

This time, Smith got the role he wanted. *Bad Boys* began filming in 1994. The themes were straight-forward—good against evil, and opposites attract. The plot had twists and turns, but basically involved finding the thieves who had stolen $100 million worth of illegal drugs from a police station's evidence room.

Much of the humor came out of the main characters' personalities. These two police officers and partners are polar opposites of one another. Lawrence, as Marcus Burnett, is a conservative family man. Smith, as Mike Lowrey, is a bachelor with a wild private life.

To prepare for the role of Mike Lowrey, Smith bulked up by working out in a gym. He enjoyed his new image. "*Bad Boys* was the first time in my life that I can remember people looking at me as physically attractive," he said. "I've always been kinda goofy-looking. Thin and lanky and big ears and all of that."[2]

Smith was by now experienced enough to know that making a movie was not easy work. However, shooting *Bad Boys* was especially grueling because the movie is set in Miami and part of the shooting had to be done in the middle of the hot, sticky summer.

There are a lot of explosions in *Bad Boys*, with a garbage truck, an airplane, and several cars being blown up. Movie scenes tend to be reshot several times until the director is satisfied. However, it would have cost far too much to redo complicated scenes involving explosions. So there was a lot of pressure on Smith, Lawrence, and the crew to get them just right on the first take.

Bad Boys was a major step in Smith's movie career, but he still had a television show to make. *The Fresh Prince of Bel-Air* began its fifth season in September 1994. Smith became the show's coproducer, along with Benny Medina.

The Fresh Prince of Bel-Air reached a milestone when its one hundredth new episode was aired on September 19, 1994. The episode was titled, "What's Will Got to Do With It?"—a takeoff on a famous song by singer Tina Turner: "What's Love Got to Do With It?" The plot centered on Will's trying to manage the singing career of a rising young star, his cousin Ashley. In a statement to the press marking the one hundredth episode, Smith said that he wanted to act in another hundred episodes and make them as good as the first hundred.

By that time, several other African-American actors were starring in weekly television series. Medina praised Smith's example, saying, "Will opened the door for a lot of young black artists and performers, like Martin [Lawrence] and Queen Latifah, to enter a formerly conservative medium."[3]

As for his personal life, Smith wanted to spend as much time with Trey as possible. He brought his son to the set of *The Fresh Prince of Bel-Air*, where the rest of the cast thought he was a cute and well-behaved child. When the cameras started rolling, Trey would put his finger on his lips and whisper "Shhhh."

But Smith's sixteen-hour workdays were putting too much stress on his marriage. Smith later said, "We had a new son, and my career was taking off. There was a lot of pressure that didn't allow the marriage to blossom. You know how you're on the freeway and you see that one car on the side of the road? Thousands of cars drive by it. Well, every once in a while it's your turn to be broken down. And you wait for the tow truck to come. That's how I viewed that difficult time in my life."[4] Will and Sheree Smith officially separated early in 1995 and divorced later that year.

In contrast to his personal problems, Smith's career was on the rise. *Bad Boys*, released in May 1995, was a big hit, taking in $215 million in ticket sales in the United States and overseas combined.[5] The movie also received generally positive reviews. Critics had praise for both Smith and Lawrence, saying they reacted well to each other's lines and played perfectly off one another's actions. The critic for *Rolling Stone* magazine wrote, "The climactic shootout inside an airplane hangar, complete with a 727 blowing sky high, slides the film into overdrive. It's all special-effects noise and nonsense. We're not fooled. Lawrence and Smith are the real firecrackers."[6] In Martin Lawrence, Smith found not only a reliable costar but also a lifelong friend.

Another person was about to become important in Smith's life. He had known Jada Pinkett for some time. They had first met in 1990 during the first season of *Fresh Prince*. A well-known actress, she had appeared in several hit movies, including *Menace II Society, Jason's Lyric, The Nutty Professor*, and *A Low Down Dirty Shame*. Pinkett auditioned to play Will's girlfriend on *Fresh Prince*, but she was rejected for the part. Standing just over five feet tall, Pinkett was considered too short to be Smith's girlfriend.

In real life, however, Smith and Pinkett worked together just fine. After she was turned down for the role on *Fresh Prince*, Jada and Will stayed in touch and became close friends. Like Smith, Pinkett is from the East Coast (Baltimore, Maryland) and grew up in a middle-class family. Her father was a contractor, and her mother was a nurse. As an actor, she understands the long hours and dedication one must put in to do the job. In Smith's opinion, her understanding of him goes far beyond their shared pursuit of a career in acting. "She's really insightful," he has said. "It was exciting and new for me to have questions I felt only she could answer. I found myself disappointed when I couldn't talk to her, when it was late or she was working."[7]

After Will and Jada's friendship blossomed into romance, she moved into his sprawling ranch house, nicknamed La Hacienda (large estate). Unlike many actors, Smith had not settled in Beverly Hills or Bel-Air. He thought it would be better to raise a family away from the show business community. La Hacienda is in the town of Thousand Oaks, about twenty miles from Beverly Hills. The majority of his neighbors do not work in show business.

On television, Smith was about to say farewell to Bel-Air. The 1995–1996 season of *The Fresh Prince of Bel-Air* would be the show's last. Smith's prediction that he would do a second hundred shows would fall far short. But he believed the time was right for him to leave *The Fresh Prince of Bel-Air*.

The decision was not easy. The show was built around Will's character, and it would be impossible for it to continue without him. Television is a business, and Smith knew his decision would hurt his costars and the crew. When the show ended, they would be out of work. However, from an artistic standpoint, Smith felt *The Fresh Prince of Bel-Air* had gone about as far as it could go. It seemed as if all the storylines had already been done. The show was starting to get stale.

Only twenty years old when the series premiered, Smith was now twenty-six. His character had spent six years living in Bel-Air. He did not think he could continue to realistically play a young man who did not fit in. Smith was no longer the Fresh Prince. From now on, he would use his real name, Will Smith.

After his success in *Bad Boys*, Smith had become an actor in demand. Not only is he talented; but he attracts fans of different races and age groups. To movie producers, popular actors are reliable moneymakers.

After playing a con artist and a police officer in his two previous movies, Smith was ready for another challenge. He was delighted to be asked to play a lead in a science fiction movie to be titled *Independence Day*. It was something he had always wanted to do.

Independence Day is another good-versus-evil movie. Aliens invade the earth, causing death and destruction. It is up to a handful of heroes to save the planet: the president of the United States, played by Bill Pullman; a brainy computer nerd, played by Jeff Goldblum; and a pilot from the United States Marine Corps, played by Will Smith.

Bonneville Salt Flats

The Bonneville Salt Flats are a barren, white stretch of land that seems to have been transported to Earth from another world. The area consists of about thirty thousand acres of salt crust atop soft mud on what was an ancient lake. Because the land is almost perfectly flat, it is used by high-speed auto racers for test drives. In 1970, a rocket car driven by racer Gary Gabolich reached an amazing 622.4 miles per hour on the flats. Many moviemakers come to this bizarre landscape to shoot films—especially those with a science-fiction theme.

Independence Day is filled with special effects, drama, and some wise-guy humor. When Smith's character, Captain Steve Hiller, is called to the rescue, he boasts that he is off to "kick ET's butt." At one point in the movie, he punches out an evil alien, saying with a deadpan expression, "Welcome to earth."

To prepare for the role in *Independence Day*, Smith met with a marine lieutenant to study the basic technique of flying an F-16. The marines let him try their virtual-reality simulator, which gave Smith the experience of flying a fighter jet while never leaving the ground. He again worked with a personal trainer to become more muscular.

The filming of *Independence Day* provided some real challenges. The first day of shooting took place in the summer of 1995 in one of the hottest places on earth—the Bonneville Salt Flats in the desert near the Utah–Nevada border. The daytime temperature there averaged 120° F.

The acting for this movie was tricky, too. Sometimes Smith's character appears in scenes with the aliens. However, the aliens were actually computer-generated and added to the movie after the scenes were filmed. So when Captain Steve Hiller is supposed to be interacting with an alien, Smith was filmed standing by himself and talking to a mark on the ground. Later, the alien would be placed on that mark. Acting opposite a blank space was a challenge for Smith.

Once he was finished filming *Independence Day*, Smith had to wrap up the last episodes of The *Fresh Prince of Bel-Air*. After the final show was taped in March 1996, the cast celebrated with a wrap party. Will could not resist acting like a teenager again. Things got out of hand when he started a friendly cake fight. The rest of the cast got into it, and soon they all ended up with icing and crumbs on their faces and hair.

In the last episode, broadcast on May 20, 1996, the Banks family sells its mansion and moves back to Philadelphia. Will is the only family member who stays in Los Angeles, to finish college. In a clever touch, the Bankses show their house to potential buyers that include characters from old television comedies such as *Diff'rent Strokes* (which ran from 1978 to 1986) and The Jeffersons (1975–1985).

The Fresh Prince of Bel-Air was never a huge hit, but it was a solid one. A total of 148 episodes were broadcast.[8] The show was televised not only in North America but in more than ten other countries, including Spain (where it was called *El Principe de Bel-Air*), Croatia (*Princ s Bel-Aira*), Israel (*Hanasih Hamadlik MiBel-Air*) and Denmark (*Rap fyr I L.A.*). Reruns of the show were shown on the Nickelodeon Network's nighttime programming segment Nick at Nite until 2009. After that, ABC Family began airing the reruns.

While *The Fresh Prince of Bel-Air* was first and foremost a comedy, Smith later said that his favorite episodes were the ones dealing with serious issues: "From the fan mail I've received, I know the show helped many teens get through difficult situations. Even if we couldn't offer them solutions, our show had shown them that they're not alone."[9]

Chapter 7

TECH JUNKIE SUPERSTAR

I t was only natural that *Independence Day* would open in theaters across the United States on Independence Day weekend. Instead of watching fireworks in 1996, it seemed that everyone was at the movies. *Independence Day* was huge. Action move fans felt this was a movie they must see. Over its first five days, *Independence Day* earned $83.5 million in ticket sales, setting a new record for the most money any movie had earned in such a short period.[1] Fans went to see *Independence Day* again and again. By the end of 1996, the movie had earned more than $300 million, and Smith was a full-fledged star. He joked about his status as a movie hero after the success of *Independence Day*: "I'm probably the first black guy who ever saved the world."[2]

While audiences were caught up in the thrills of *Independence Day*, Smith was already filming his next movie, another science-fiction film about aliens: *Men in Black*. Both *Independence Day* and *Men in Black* are about aliens, but they are distinctly different films. *Independence Day* is mainly science fiction with dashes of comedy thrown in. *Men in Black* is an over-the-top comedy that happens to be science fiction. The aliens are not poised and ready to attack planet Earth. In fact, they have been living on Earth for years. It is these aliens, not humans, who actually invented the gadgets humans take for granted, such as microwave ovens and Velcro.

In *Men in Black*, Smith plays New York City policeman James D. Edwards III, known as Agent J. He is teamed up with a partner, Agent K, played by actor Tommy Lee Jones. The two become part of a special force called the Men in Black, whose job is to monitor alien activity on Earth. Before long, the two agents are fighting two groups of terrorist aliens who want to destroy each other, using Earth as the battlefield.

Men in Black has plenty of vibrant and sometimes gross special effects. In one scene, a giant alien bug explodes all over Agents J and K, and they are covered in slime. The slime used on Smith and Jones during the filming was a gooey glycerin syrup mixed with food particles.

Like Smith's previous action hit, *Men in Black* opened on Independence Day weekend. Also like *Independence Day*, *Men in Black* was a smash hit and it earned more money than any other movie for the entire year of 1997.[3] The reviews for both Smith and Jones were superb. The movie gave rise to a fashion fad, as young people everywhere dressed in black and donned Ray-Ban sunglasses to look like Agents J and K. On top of that, a toy company produced *Men in Black* action figures.

Men in Black had one additional bonus. It revived Smith's music career, which had slowed down. Smith performed the movie's theme song, a rap number titled "Men in Black." Smith was now a solo artist, performing under his real name.

For four weeks in the summer of 1997, *Billboard* magazine's charts ranked the movie's theme song as number one across the United States in radio airplay.[4] Smith included the song on his first solo album, *Big Willie Style*, which was released in November.

What did Smith mean by *Big Willie Style*? "A Willie is someone who is great at something," said Smith. "Michael Jordan, for instance, is a basketball Willie."[5] Another time he said, "Being a Big Willie is not about what kind of car you drive, it's not really that. Being a Willie is in your attitude."[6] Smith further explained that being brainy has a lot to do with it. "For me, the ultimate Willie tool, the Willie measuring stick, the Willie litmus test is intellect."[7]

Unlike some celebrities, Smith is not standoffish. He appreciates his fans and tries not to ignore them. In an online computer chat on December 23, 1997, one of Smith's fans asked which movie was more fun to make: *Independence Day* or *Men in Black*. Smith's reply offered a peek behind the scenes: "They were both fun, but making special effects movies, in general, isn't something that you'd consider fun. It's hard work. There's stunts, and when you're working with special effects, there's a lot of hours of just sitting around. The real fun is going to the premiere and sitting with the audience and watching if people like it."[8] When asked about roles he would like to play in the future, Smith said, "The concept for me to play [boxer] Muhammad Ali came up. I'd love to do that story but I'd have to see a wonderful script."[9]

Sticking by Smith's side through his journey to stardom was his girlfriend Jada Pinkett. After being together for more than two years, the two actors married on New Year's Eve, 1997. Smith told a reporter, "Outside of my mother, Jada's the first person with whom I can share what I think and what I feel so freely."[10] Jada expressed a similar feeling about Will. "There is nothing that I can't share with him," she said. "That doesn't mean that this is perfect, but it's the closest thing to perfect you can get."[11]

During the wedding reception, a disc jockey spun records for the guests, just as Jazzy Jeff had done for the Fresh Prince many years ago in Philadelphia. Smith could not let go of the rapper inside himself. At one point, he jumped onstage with his five-year-old son, Trey. Together, the two of them sang Smith's next hit single from *Big Willie Style*, "Gettin' Jiggy Wit It." This song, too, became a number-one hit.

Smith spent much of early 1998 shooting his next film, *Enemy of the State*. He plays Robert Clayton Dean, a Washington, D.C., lawyer who is living a normal, uneventful life until he accidentally receives key evidence about a serious crime. Suddenly, Dean finds himself caught in a dangerous web of politics and intrigue.

Smith was the sole lead in *Enemy of the State*. He did not have a costar to fall back on, as he had in his three previous films. In addition, although the movie included some car chases and other action scenes, there were no real special effects to carry the film. The main responsibility for the movie's success was on Smith's shoulders.

In February, Smith captured his third Grammy Award, his first as a solo performer. It was for best rap solo performance for the song "Men in Black." On July 8 there was more excitement in the Smith-Pinkett household when Jada gave birth to Smith's second child, a son they named Jaden Christopher Syre Smith.

Enemy of the State was released in November 1998. It was not a blockbuster like *Independence Day* and *Men in Black*, but was still a success. Critics gave the movie mixed reviews, but fans loved it. Six months after it was released, *Enemy of the State* had made about $250 million.[12]

In February 1999, Smith earned his fourth Grammy. It was for best rap performance for his recording "Gettin' Jiggy Wit It."

Like *Independence Day* and *Men in Black*, Smith's next feature, *Wild, Wild West* was released on a Fourth of July weekend. Because so many of his movies opened on that holiday, Smith had morphed from the prince into a king: the king of the Fourth of July.

Wild, Wild West was based on a television program that had aired from 1965 to 1969—a western with a James Bond touch. The title refers not only to the Old West but to the main character, James T. West, played by Smith. He and his partner, Artemus Gordon, played by Kevin Kline, fight evil with unusual gadgets rather than ordinary six-shooters. Like James Bond, James T. West is handsome and charming. His sidekick, Gordon, is a master of disguises and trickery.

It is said that all hot streaks come to an end. The critics were almost unanimous in their reviews of *Wild, Wild West*. Nearly all hated it. Some said the plot was weak. Others said the movie relied so much on gadgets that it was distracting. Still others complained that the characters were not well developed. Another criticism of this film was that there were too many jokes about West being African-American, and that most of them were not funny. In the newspaper *USA Today*, movie reviewer Susan Wloszczyna summed up the general feeling when she called *Wild, Wild West* "a wild, wild mess."[13]

Few critics found fault with either Smith's or Kline's performance, saying that the actors were not given good material to work with. For Smith, the one bright spot regarding *Wild, Wild West* was his recording of the movie's theme song. It reached number one on the national sales charts in the summer of 1999.[14]

Between shooting movies, Smith returned to the recording studio to make more music. Sometimes he drew on current events for inspiration. In the summer of 1999, nobody could turn on a television news broadcast without hearing about the year 2000, the first year in a new millennium (a period of one thousand years). The abbreviation for one thousand is the letter K, which stands for the metric kilo, so people called the upcoming year Y2K for short.

In a play on words, Smith titled his new album *Willennium.* It was released in November 1999. "I wanted to cover the last fifteen years of my career," Smith said. "I essentially wanted to make an album that covered the gamut of the lifestyle I've led and am leading. The album has real old-school on it, including the way me and [Jazzy] Jeff used to rock, and then it has some songs that come into my new flavor. I'm 31 years old, so I'm talking about different things now with more mature concepts."[15]

One song on *Willennium*, which Smith sings with Jada, is called "Afro Angel." It talks about the temptations of drugs and sex in the inner city. In another song, "The Rain," the subject is the recklessness of Smith's early years in the music business. The topic may be weighty, but Smith did not resort to profanity. He explained, "You can be more aggressive without being profane. I could easily

The Razzies

Every year, a group of movie critics presents the Golden Raspberry Awards, known as the Razzies. These awards are given to the worst movies and performances of the previous year. The Razzies are a humorous counterpart to the Academy Awards, or Oscars. The Academy Awards are presented by the Academy of Motion Picture Arts and Sciences to the year's best movies and performances. Winning an Oscar is one of the biggest thrills an actor can achieve. The Razzies are meant to be satire. Newspapers and television networks regularly report on movie critics' annual selections.

write an album full of profane records. But that's way too easy. I challenge profane rappers to do what I do—write an album full of non-profane records."[16]

Despite the album's more serious material, the first single from *Willennium* was a lighthearted number, "Will 2K." This fun song about the excitement of waiting for the year 2000 became a moderate hit.

In the entertainment business, Smith was by now in the big leagues. Like the athletes in the major leagues, stars must be thick-skinned. Smith was about to be tested. Early in 2000, he learned that he was the so-called winner of a Razzie award.

For the Razzies in 2000, *Wild, Wild West* was selected as the worst movie of 1999. Will Smith and Kevin Kline were named the worst screen couple. And even though the movie's title song had won Smith another Grammy Award and earned a Gold Record for selling five hundred thousand copies, it was chosen for a Razzie as the worst original song from a movie. Needless to say, neither Smith nor Klein came to the Razzie ceremony. Instead, Robert Conrad, who had played James T. West in the old television series, showed up to accept the award. Sarcastically, he said, "I can't tell you how happy this makes me."[17]

In spite of the terrible things critics said about *Wild, Wild West*, it still attracted enough moviegoers to make a profit. Plenty of people went to see it—and Smith was not about to let one critical failure set him back. He continued taking risks.

Chapter 8

GOLF AND BACK TO *MEN IN BLACK*

S mith's next movie was a departure from *Men in Black*, *Independence Day*, and *Wild, Wild West*. They had no splashy special effects, no wild gadgets, and no booming explosions. Instead, *The Legend of Bagger Vance* is a drama set in Savannah, Georgia, during the Great Depression of the 1930s. Smith plays Bagger Vance, a mystical caddy who teams up with a golfer named Rannulph Junuh, played by Matt Damon. The fictional Junuh is a once-great golfer whose career has been ruined by alcohol abuse.

Bagger Vance is as much a philosopher as he is a caddy. Much of his advice to Junuh about golf can also be applied to life in general. Smith was pleased to be in a movie about golf. "Golf is the ultimate sport," he said. "It's the perfect blend of physical ability and mental prowess."[1]

The Legend of Bagger Vance premiered in November 2000, but no one could fault Smith if he had other things on his mind. On October 31, 2000, Jada gave birth to their daughter, Willow Camille Reign Smith. Halloween was a fitting birthday for the daughter of a science-fiction fan.

The Legend of Bagger Vance received mixed reviews. The movie is set in the Deep South at a time when racial segregation was enforced by law. While some critics had complained about the heavy racial commentary in *Wild, Wild West*, a number of reviewers griped that *The Legend of Bagger Vance* barely touched on the issue. Still, as with Smith's previous movies, enough moviegoers saw *The Legend of Bagger Vance* to earn it a profit.

Back in 1997 Smith had said that he would like to play Muhammad Ali, but only if a wonderful script came along. One did, and in 2001 he took on the title role in *Ali*. Several critics believed that for Smith, it was the role of a lifetime. Yet he confessed that it was an intimidating part. "I didn't want to be the dude that messed up the Muhammad Ali story," he said.[2]

Ali had been drafted to serve in the United States army during the Vietnam War, but he refused to become a soldier. He said that according to his strict religious beliefs, war is immoral. Taking a stand against war made Ali a hero to some people, a villain to others. The United States government stripped Ali of his boxing license and his

Muhammad Ali

Muhammad Ali is ranked as one of the greatest boxers of all time and is one of the world's most famous athletes. Yet he is also one of the most controversial sports figures in American history. Ali's original name was Cassius Clay. In 1964, he joined the Nation of Islam, a religious group also known as Black Muslims, and changed his name to Muhammad Ali. During his career as a fighter, Ali was the first boxer to win the heavyweight title three times: in 1964, 1974, and 1978. Ali retired from boxing in 1981, and despite the limitations of Parkinson's syndrome, he has devoted his time and energy to raising money for charities and working for world peace.

heavyweight title, but Ali still did not back down. Eventually, the Supreme Court ruled in Ali's favor, and he regained his license and his title.

Tall and lanky by nature, Smith does not naturally have the solid build of a professional boxer. To try to resemble Ali as much as possible, Smith took on a rigorous workout schedule with a professional trainer for twelve months. "We would run at 6 A.M., three to five miles, depending on the day," said Smith. "We'd go to the gym from 10:30 A.M. to 1:30 P.M. and do technical boxing training, jumping rope, and sparring. And in the evenings we'd do weight training. That was five or six days a week for a year, so your body will definitely come into shape with that kind of regimen."[3]

The hard work combined with Smith's natural talent paid off. The movie was a success, and Smith received a nomination for an Academy Award for best lead actor in a movie. It was payback for the Razzie award earned by *Wild, Wild West*. Although the Oscar for best actor in 2002 went to Denzel Washington, being nominated for this role was an honor for Smith. It proved that he was being taken seriously by others in the movie industry.

In 2002 Smith released another solo album, *Born to Reign*, which included songs about his wife and children. In one number, he confesses that his daughter, Willow, has him wrapped around her finger. The album also explores musical styles that are different from old-school hip-hop. One song is Latin-flavored; another has a reggae influence. Even though he had hit the big time as a movie star, Smith said in 2002, "I really do still consider myself a rapper first."[4]

Smith teamed up with a couple of past partners for his next two movies, both of which were sequels. In 2002 he starred with Tommy Lee Jones in *Men in Black II*. In 2003, Smith and Martin Lawrence joined up again for *Bad Boys II*. Both movies received a wide range of reviews. As is typical with sequels, most critics who liked the original movies thought the follow-ups were not as good. Still, like most of Smith's movies, both of these drew plenty of viewers.

Smith has continued his practice of starring in one big movie per year. He returned to his favorite genre, science fiction, and combined it with mystery in *I, Robot*, released in 2004. *I, Robot* is based on the writings of the renowned science-fiction writer Isaac Asimov. Smith plays a police officer in 2035 called to investigate a murder that took place in a robot factory. A question arises: Are robots trying to take over the world?

In the movie, Smith's character is scared of technology. Smith is just the opposite. He proudly admits, "I'm a tech junkie."[5] He had fun with the special effects used in *I, Robot*. The staff used human expressions, body language, and voices to make the robots seem real. Smith explained, "So, there's a real human quality to the robots that are really fun for me, but I think will be chilling for people watching the movie."[6]

Most reviews for *I, Robot* were positive. Movie critic Michael Wilmington of *The Chicago Tribune* called the film "a high-tech thriller that really works—both because of its eye-popping visual feats and the ideas and humanity behind them."[7]

Smith continued to try new things. He did the voice for one of the characters in the animated movie *Shark Tale*, released in 2004, and took on his first starring role in a romantic comedy, *Hitch*, which opened in time for Valentine's Day, 2005. Smith's character in *Hitch* is Alex Hitchins. His job is to give dating advice, but he makes one blunder after another in his own attempt to win the heart of a gossip columnist, played by actress Eva Mendes.

Smith passed the test in the genre of romantic comedy. Audiences flocked to the theaters, making the movie number one for the first couple of weeks after it was released. Most critics liked it, too. Reviewer Carina Chocano, in the *Los Angeles Times*, wrote, "Smith is a gifted comic actor, and seeing him in a lighthearted comedy, his first romantic lead, is a pure pleasure."[8]

Smith released another solo album, *Lost and Found*, in March 2005. He explores difficult subjects such as religious fanaticism and having to explain the terrorist attacks of September 11, 2001, to his son. Still, Smith maintains his signature pop-rap style through most of the album. The opening song, "Here He Comes," plays with the original *Spider-Man* theme. Another song, "Nice Guy," counters rap star Eminem's criticism of Smith's music.

Lost and Found has seen more success than his previous effort, *Born to Reign*. Smith admits that his acting career has affected his development as a musician. However, he says that his music career is finally taking a turn: "I've had more life experience. . . . I think lyrically I'm much more prepared than I've ever been before."[9]

In 2006, Will Smith got to costar with his son, Jaden, in the movie *The Pursuit of Happyness*, about a father and son who end up homeless, but manage to survive because of their love for each other and the father's tenacity. Two years later, Smith got to do another science fiction movie. This one was called *Hancock*, and it was about a man with superpowers who is not a completely good person. That same decade, Smith starred in *I Am Legend* (2007), a vampire movie, and *Seven Pounds* (2008), about a man who is seeking redemption after he causes a fatal car wreck. Then he began work on *Men in Black III* (2012).

Today, Will Smith is one of the kings of the entertainment industry—both in popularity and in earnings. In June 2008, *Forbes*, a top business magazine, had estimated that he earned $80 million in the previous year alone.[10] That same year, he was selected by TV host Barbara Walters as one of the most fascinating people of 2008.

Some of Smith's fellow actors say that in addition to his natural talent, Smith's confidence sets him apart. Regina King, who acted with Smith *in Enemy of the State*, observed, "If Will Smith worked at Subway, he'd still love himself. He'd be the best sandwich maker there, and he'd tell you about it: 'When I make my turkey and cheese sandwich, see, I melt the cheese!' He's so proud of whatever he does, and I love that."[11]

In the world of entertainment, where some actors never hit the big time, and others do not make it until they have been in movies for twenty years or more, Will Smith is still a young man. In spite of his youth, he has achieved success in many areas of the performing arts.

How will Smith be remembered years from now? As a pioneer rapper? As a comic television actor who, thanks to the power of reruns, will forever be regarded as the Fresh Prince? As a movie-star action hero? As a leading man? All of the above? Or perhaps Smith will reign in the future as a king of some genre of entertainment he has not yet tried. Only time will tell.

CHRONOLOGY

1968—Willard Christopher Smith Jr. is born September 25 in Philadelphia, Pennsylvania.

1973—Begins attending Our Lady of Lourdes school.

1980—Starts rapping as a hobby.

1982—Enters Overbrook High School.

1984—Meets future partner Jeff Townes.

1987—As DJ Jazzy Jeff and the Fresh Prince, Smith and Townes release their first song, "Girls Ain't Nothing But Trouble," and release their first album, *Rock the House*.

1988—Their breakthrough album, *He's the DJ, I'm the Rapper*, is released.

1989—Smith and Townes win a Grammy Award for best rap performance; third album, *And In This Corner...*, is released.

1990–1996—Smith stars in television situation comedy *The Fresh Prince of Bel-Air*.

1991—The album *Homebase* is released.

1992—Smith and Townes win a Grammy for best rap song, "Summertime"; Smith has his first movie role, in *Where the Day Takes You*; marries Sheree Zampino on May 9; son Willard Christopher Smith III (Trey) is born in December.

1993—Appears in movies *Made in America* and *Six Degrees of Separation*; fifth album with DJ Jazzy Jeff, *Code Red*, is released.

1995—Costars in *Bad Boys*; is divorced from Sherry Zampino.

1996—Costars in *Independence Day*.

1997—Stars in *Men in Black*; first solo album, *Big Willie Style*, is released; Smith marries Jada Pinkett on December 31.

1998—Wins first solo Grammy; son Jaden Christopher Syre Smith is born on July 8; Smith stars in *Enemy of the State*.

1999—Wins second solo Grammy; stars in *Wild, Wild West*; second solo album, *Willennium*, is released.

2000—Daughter, Willow Camille Reign Smith, is born on October 31; stars in *Legend of Bagger Vance*.

2001—Stars in *Ali*.

2002—Receives Academy Award nomination for *Ali*, but does not win; stars in *Men in Black II*; third solo album, *Born to Reign*, is released.

2003—Costars in *Bad Boys II*.

2004—Stars in *I, Robot*; does voice-over in the animated movie *Shark Tale*.

2005—Stars in *Hitch*; fourth solo album, *Lost and Found*, is released.

2006—Stars in *The Pursuit of Happyness*.

2007—Stars in *I Am Legend*.

2008—Stars in *Hancock* and *Seven Pounds*; is named one of 2008's most fascinating people by Barbara Walters.

2012—Stars in *Men in Black III*.

DISCOGRAPHY & FILMOGRAPHY

DJ Jazzy Jeff and the Fresh Prince

Albums and Compact Discs

Rock the House, 1987	Gold Record
He's the DJ, I'm the Rapper, 1988	3x Platinum Record
And in This Corner . . . , 1989	Gold Record
Homebase, 1991	Platinum Record
Code Red, 1993	Gold Record
Greatest Hits, 1998	

Singles

"Girls Ain't Nothing But Trouble," 1987	
"Parents Just Don't Understand," 1988	Gold Record
"A Nightmare on My Street," 1988	
"Summertime," 1991	Platinum Record
"Ring My Bell," 1991	Gold Record
"Boom! Shake the Room," 1993	

Will Smith
Albums and Compact Discs

Big Willie Style, 1997	9x Platinum Record
Willennium, 1999	Double Platinum Record
Born to Reign, 2002	Gold Record
Greatest Hits, 2002	
Lost and Found, 2005	

Singles

"Gettin' Jiggy Wit It," 1998	
"Just the Two of Us," 1998	Gold Record
"Wild, Wild West," 1999	
"Will 2K," 1999	Gold Record

Movies

Where the Day Takes You, 1992

Made in America, 1993

Six Degrees of Separation, 1993

Bad Boys, 1995

Independence Day, 1996

Men in Black, 1997

Enemy of the State, 1998

Wild, Wild West, 1999

The Legend of Bagger Vance, 2000

Ali, 2001

Men in Black II, 2002

Movies (continued)

Bad Boys II, 2003

I, Robot, 2004

Shark Tale, 2004 (voice-over)

Hitch, 2005

The Pursuit of Happyness, 2006

I Am Legend, 2007

Hancock, 2008

Seven Pounds, 2008

Men in Black III, 2012

Television

The Fresh Prince of Bel-Air (1990–1996)

CHAPTER NOTES

Chapter 1. Rappin' Into History

1. "What Is Rap?" Rap Realm, BBC Web site, <http://www.bbc.co.uk/education/listenandwrite/raprealm/whatisr.htm> (January 7, 2005).

2. David Handelman, "Rock & Roll . . . and Justice for Few," *Rolling Stone*, April 6, 1989, p. 45.

3. Ibid.

4. Jan Berenson, *Will Power: A Biography of Will Smith* (New York: Pocket Books, 1997), p. 33.

Chapter 2. Getting Paid to Party

1. Jan Berenson, *Will Power: A Biography of Will Smith* (New York: Pocket Books, 1997), p. 5.

2. Nancy Collins, "Will Smith," *Rolling Stone*, December 10, 1998, <http://www.rollingstone.com> (December 8, 2004).

3. Ibid.

4. Brian J. Robb, *Will Smith: King of Cool* (London: Plexus Publishing Ltd., 2000), p. 13.

5. Ibid., p.10.

6. K.S. Rodriguez, *Will Smith: From Fresh Prince to King of Cool* (New York: HarperCollins, 1998), p. 10.

7. "Will Smith Q&A," *London Mirror*, August 5, 2004, <http://www.mirror.co.uk> (December 8, 2004).

8. Rodriguez, pp. 9–10.

9. Collins.

10. "An Interview with Will Smith," Handbag.com Web site, <http:www.handbag.com/gossip/celebrityinterviews/willsmith2> (December 8, 2004).

11. Joel Whitburn, *The Billboard Book of Top 40 Hits* (New York: Billboard Books, 2004), p. 612.

12. Janet Cawley, "Topping the Charts and Saving the World: Will Smith," *Biography*, July 1999, downloaded from EBSCOhost (December 6, 2004).

13. Robb, p. 17.

14. Ibid., p. 18.

15. Chris Nickson, *Will Smith* (New York: St. Martin's Press, 1999), p. 18.

16. Berenson, p. 16.

17. "Will Smith—My Granny Told Me Off for Swearing," BBC Worldwide Press, July 22, 2002, <http://www.bbc.co.uk/pressoffice/commercial/worldwidestories/pressreleases/2002/07_jul> (December 7, 2004).

18. David Ritz, "Will Power," *Essence*, February 1993, downloaded from EBSCOhost (December 6, 2004).

19. Nickson, p. 19.

Chapter 3. He's the DJ, I'm the Rapper

1. Chris Nickson, *Will Smith* (New York: St. Martin's Press, 1999), p. 26.

2. AOL Chat, December 23, 1997, reproduced on <http://jazzyjefffreshprince.com> (January 18, 2005).

3. Jan Berenson, *Will Power: A Biography of Will Smith* (New York: Pocket Books, 1997), p. 23.

4. Brian J. Robb, *Will Smith: King of Cool* (London: Plexus Publishing Ltd., 2000), p. 27.

5. Berenson, pp. 23–24.

6. "Introducing . . . Jazzy Jeff and Fresh Prince, Rap's More Mild Than Wild Guys," *People*, October 3, 1988, < http://jazzyjefffreshprince.com> (January 17, 2005).

7. "Willennium Extravaganza," 1999, <http://jazzyjefffreshprince.com> (January 18, 2005).

8. Joel Whitburn, *The Billboard Book of Top 40 Hits* (New York: Billboard Books, 2000), p. 547.

9. Nickson, p. 27.

10. Robb, p. 27.

11. "Jazzy Jeff Interview," Defected Records, originally appeared on bonus disc of Jazzy Jeff's album *In The House* <http://jazzyjefffreshprince.com> (January 18, 2005).

12. Whitburn, p. 191.

13. Robb, p. 32.

14. Berenson, p. 34.

15. Robb, p. 32.

16. "Stars' Secret Pleasures," *The Tribune* "Sunday Extra," December 11, 2004, <http://www.tribuneindia.com/2004/20041211/saturday/main5.htm> (January 22, 2005).

17. K. S. Rodriguez, *Will Smith: From Fresh Prince to King of Cool* (New York: HarperCollins, 1998), p. 21.

18. William Leith, "Big Ears Flies Again," *Mail & Guardian*, February 4, 1999, <http://www.chico.mweb.co.za/mg/art/film/9902/990204-smith.html> (January 22, 2005).

Chapter 4. From Rapper to Actor

1. Jan Berenson, *Will Power: A Biography of Will Smith* (New York: Pocket Books, 1997), p. 45.

2. Chris Nickson, *Will Smith* (New York: St. Martin's Press, 1999), p. 45.

3. Berenson, p. 45.

4. Jeffrey Ressner, "Raps to Riches," *Rolling Stone*, September 20, 1990, p. 45.

5. Ed Siegel, "*Buck* Will Have Tough Time Beating Prince's Rap," *The Boston Globe*, September 10, 1990, p. 38.

6. Larry Rohter, "'Fresh Prince of Bel-Air' Puts Rap in Mainstream," *New York Times*, September 17, 1990, p. C17.

7. John J. O'Connor, "Black Sitcoms Steeped in Concept," *New York Times*, October 4, 1990, p. C26.

8. Berenson., p. 52.

9. Aldore Collier, "Rap Star Finds TV Fame as 'Fresh Prince of Bel-Air.'" *Jet*, December 3, 1990, p. 62.

10. Ressner.

11. Donald Clarke, "Will's Power," *The Irish Times*, August 6, 2004, <http://www.ireland.com/theticket/articles/2004/0806/4015223511TK0 608WILLSMITH.html> (December 8, 2004).

Chapter 5. Six Degrees of the Fresh Prince

1. Aldore Collier, "Rap Star Finds TV Fame as 'Fresh Prince of Bel-Air.'" *Jet*, December 3, 1990, p. 62.

2. Ibid.

3. Joel Whitburn, *The Billboard Book of Top 40 Hits* (New York: Billboard Books, 2000), p. 191; J.R. Reynolds, "The Rhythm and the Blues," *Billboard*, September 24, 1994, downloaded from EBSCOhost (December 6, 2004).

4. A.D. Amorosi, "Made From Scratch," citypaper.net, August 13, 2002, <http://jazzyjefffreshprince.com/jjfp-intjjcitypaper.htm> (January 18, 2005).

5. J.R. Reynolds, "'Fresh Prince' a Watershed for Hip-Hop and African-Americans in General on TV," *Billboard*, September 24, 1994, downloaded from EBSCOhost (December 6, 2004).

6. Whitburn, p. 191.

7. Tim Brooks and Earle Marsh, *The Complete Directory to Prime Time Network and Cable TV Shows* (New York: Ballantine Books, 1999), p. 1257.

8. Ben Falk, "*Six Degrees of Separation* (1993)," BBC web site, March 19, 2001, <htt;://www.bbc.co.uk/films/2001/03/19/six_degrees_of_separation> (February 9, 2005).

9. Ibid.

10. Rita Kempley, "Six Degrees of Separation," *Washington Post*, December 22, 1993, <http://www.washingtonpost.com> (February 9, 2005).

11. Janet Maslin, "Review/Film: *Six Degrees of Separation*; John Guare's 'Six Degrees,' on Art and Life Stories, Real and Fake," *New York Times*, December 8, 1993, <http://movies2.nytimes.com> (February 9, 2005).

12. Chris Nickson, *Will Smith* (New York: St. Martin's Press, 1999), p. 77.

13. Brooks, Marsh, p. 1257.

14. Nickson, p. 79.

15. Ibid., p. 80.

16. Brian J. Robb, *Will Smith: King of Cool* (London: Plexus Publishing Ltd., 2000), p. 70.

17. Brooks, Marsh, p. 1257.

Chapter 6. Bad Boys and Alien Invaders

1. "Actor Says Hollywood 'Not Racist,'" BBC News, October 1, 2003, <http://newsvote.bbc.co.uk> (December 7, 2004).

2. William Leith, "Big Ears Flies Again," *Mail & Guardian*, February 4, 1999, <http://www.chico.mweb.co.za/mg/art/film/9902/990204-smith.html> (January 22, 2005).

3. J.R. Reynolds, "'Fresh Prince' a Watershed for Hip-Hop, and African-Americans in General on TV," *Billboard*, September 24, 1994, downloaded from EBSCOhost (December 6, 2004).

4. Gregory Cerio, Craig Thomashoff, "Mr. Smith Goes to Stardom," *People*, July 22, 1996, downloaded from EBSCOhost (December 6, 2004).

5. Jan Berenson, *Will Power: A Biography of Will Smith* (New York: Pocket Books, 1997), p. 94.

6. Peter Travers, "Bad Boys," *Rolling Stone*, May 7, 1995, <http://www.rollingstone.com/reviews/movies/_id/5948199> (June 10, 2005).

7. Dream Hampton, "Will Power," *Essence*, July 1997, downloaded from EBSCOhost (December 6, 2004).

8. "The Fresh Prince of Bel-Air," TV Tome web site, <http://www.tvtome.com/FreshPrinceof BelAir/season6.html> (February 3, 2005).

9. Brian J. Robb, *Will Smith: King of Cool* (London: Plexus Publishing Ltd., 2000), p. 85.

Chapter 7. Tech Junkie Superstar

1. Lynn Norment, "Why Will Smith Is Hollywood's Biggest Summer Attraction," *Ebony*, July 1999, downloaded from EBSCOhost (December 6, 2004).

2. Ibid.

3. Karen Thomas, "'Bad Boys' Are Buddying Up," *USA Today*, July 15, 2003, downloaded from EBSCOhost (December 7, 2004).

4. Joel Whitburn, *The Billboard Book of Top 40 Hits* (New York: Billboard Books, 2004), p. 583.

5. William Leith, "Big Ears Flies Again," *Mail & Guardian*, February 4, 1999, <http://www.chico.mweb.co.za/mg/art/film/9902/990204-smith.html> (January 22, 2005).

6. "Big Willie Style Interview," Columbia Records publicity interview, 1997, <http://jazzyjefffreshprince.com/jjfp-intwsbws97.htm> (January 18, 2005).

7. Ibid.

8. AOL Chat, December 23, 1997, <http://jazzyjefffreshprince .com> (January 18, 2005).

9. Ibid.

10. Alex Tresniowski, "Mr. Smith Takes a Bride," *People*, January 19, 1998, downloaded from EBSCOhost (December 6, 2004).

11. Ibid.

12. Norment.

13. "Wild, Wild West (1999)," sample reviews, Rotten Tomatoes web site, <http://www.rottentomatoes.com/m/wild_wild_west> (February 21, 2005).

14. Whitburn, p. 584.

15. Gail Mitchell, "Smith's Ready for the Willennium," *Billboard*, December 30, 1999, downloaded from EBSCOhost (December 7, 2004).

16. "Will Smith Releases 'Millennium Album,'" *Jet*, January 31, 2000, <http://www.findarticles.com> (October 12, 2005).

17. Booth Moore, "Raspberry Awards Salute Hollywood's Dishonor Roll," *Los Angeles Times*, © March 27, 2000, <http://www.wildwildwest. org/film/articles/razzies/razzies_art.html> (February 21, 2005).

Chapter 8. Golf and Back to Men in Black

1. Dream Hampton, "Will Power," *Essence*, July 1997, downloaded from EBSCOhost (December 6, 2004).

2. Jess Cagel, Simon Robinson, "Lord of the Ring," *Time*, December 24, 2001, downloaded from EBSCOhost (December 7, 2004).

3. Anwar Brett, interviewer; "Will Smith: Ali," February 2, 2002, BBC transcript, <http://www.bbc.co.uk/films/2002/02/07/will_smith_ali_interview.shtml> (December 7, 2004).

4. "Will Smith 'Born to Reign' Interview," NZ Girl web site, 2002, <http://www.nzgirl.co.nz/articles/1354> (February 23, 2005).

5. "Will Smith Q&A," *The Daily Mirror*, August 5, 2004, <http://www.mirror.co.uk> (December 8, 2004).

6. Ibid.

7. Michael Wilmington, "Movie Review: 'I, Robot.'" *Chicago Tribune*, N.D. <http://metromix.chicagotribune.com/movies> (February 23, 2005).

8. "Hitch: The Cure for the Common Man (2005)," *Los Angeles Times*, February 11, 2005, sample reviews, Rotten Tomatoes web site, <http://www.rottentomatoes.com/m/hitch> (February 23, 2005).

9. Shaheem Reid, with reporting by SuChin Pak, "Will Smith Chose Hollywood Over Hip-Hop, But Now He's Back," MTV News, April 1, 2005, <http://www.mtv.com/news/articles/1499418/20050401/story .jhtml> (October 12, 2005).

10. "The Celebrity 100: #11 Will Smith," *Forbes.com*, June 11, 2008, <http://www.forbes.com/lists/2008/53/celebrities08_Will-Smith_JRSR. html> (May 16, 2011).

11. Anne Marie Cruz, "Force of Will," *People*, December 6, 2004, downloaded from EBSCOhost (December 6, 2004).

FURTHER READING

Corrigan, Jim. *Will Smith*. Broomall, Pa.: Mason Crest Publishers, 2007.

Doeden, Matt: *Will Smith: Box Office Superstar*. Minneapolis, Minn.: Twenty First Century Books, 2009.

Garofoli, Wendy. *Hip-Hop History*. Mankato, Minn.: Capstone Press, 2010.

Juettner, Bonnie. *Will Smith*. San Diego, CA: Lucent Books, 2009.

Merino, Noel. *Rap Music*. Farmington Hills, Mich.: Greenhaven Press, 2009.

Stewart, Mark. *Will Smith*. Chicago, IL: Heinemann Library, 2005.

Todd, Anne M. *Will Smith: Actor*. Broomall, Pa.: Chelsea House Publishers, 2010.

INTERNET ADDRESSES

"Will Smith"
<http://www.willsmith.com/>
This is the official website for Will Smith.

"Biography.com"
<http://www.biography.com/people/will-smith-9542165>
Read a biography of Will Smith, and watch a 5-minute video presentation on his life

INDEX